FRIEDRICH NIETZSCHE, FIGHTER FOR FREEDOM

FRIEDRICH NIETZSCHE
(1844-1900)

FRIEDRICH NIETZSCHE

FIGHTER FOR FREEDOM

⚜

Rudolf Steiner

Translated from the German by
Margaret Ingram deRis

SteinerBooks

STEINERBOOKS
An imprint of Anthroposophic Press, Inc.
834 Main Street, PO Box 358
Spencertown, New York 12165
www.steinerbooks.org

Originally published by Garber Communications, 1985.

This edition copyright © 2024 by SteinerBooks.

All rights reserved. No part of this publication may be reproduced, stored in a retrieval system, or transmitted, in any form or by any means, electronic, mechanical, photocopying, recording, or otherwise, without the prior written permission of the publisher.

ISBN: 978-1-62148-338-0

CONTENTS

Foreword to the 1985 Edition 1

Introduction: Friedrich Nietzsche and Rudolf Steiner ... 11

  I. Friedrich Nietzsche, A Fighter Against his Time

      Preface to the First German Edition, 1895 39
        i. The Character 42
        ii. The Superman 64
        iii. Nietzsche's Path of Development 121

  II. The Psychology of Friedrich Nietzsche as a
     Psychopathological Problem 153

  III. Friedrich Nietzsche's Personality and Psycho-
      therapy 181

  IV. The Personality of Friedrich Nietzsche, A
      Memorial Address 201

Index 213

FOREWORD
TO THE 1985 EDITION

IN A BOOK published in 1983 (*Twentieth-Century Literary Criticism*, Vol. 10, Gale Research Company, Detroit), 83 years after his death, the best critical reviews and articles in English about Nietzsche were finally gathered together. And what a wonderful collection they are. The roll-call of contributors to this article bears witness to the influence and importance of this man: Franz Liszt; August Strindberg; George Brandes; Max Nordan; Rudolf Steiner; George Bernard Shaw; James Huneker; G. Santayana; Stefan Zweig; Karl Jaspers; Jacques Barzun; Bertrand Russell; Thomas Mann; Albert Camus; Eric Bentley; Martin Heidegger; Rollo May; Walter Kaufman and many others. And such writers as Rilke, Stefan George, Herman Hesse, Andre Gide, William Butler Yeats, were all influenced by Nietzsche's works.

To say that Nietzsche has had a crucial and decisive effect on the cultural, intellectual, psychological, artistic and social development of the Twentieth Century is to almost understate the case. But this awareness has been objectively presented and properly understood fairly recently, perhaps only in the last 40 years. During his lifetime (1844-1900), he personally suffered as much from the negative criticism as did his works.

"These were a few interpreters and critics during his lifetime who understood the significance of his ideas, both for their own times and for the Twentieth Century. Two in particular praised Nietzsche for his awareness of the cultural decay in Europe, for his insights into individual psychology, and for his studies in ethics and morality: George Brandes and Rudolf Steiner." (Page 352, Vol. 10).

Brandes, through his lectures and works on Nietzsche, was very influential while Nietzsche was still alive. Steiner, as shown in the following pages of this book, was early-on aware of the immense importance of Nietzsche's thoughts and ideas, and of his personal, psychological and spiritual development.

There are those critics who divide Nietzsche's work into three periods, each one representing a different stage in the development of his thought. Some critics argue "that the sudden shifts in his philosophical thought demonstrate the erratic nature of his intellect; others such as Rudolf Steiner, Eric Bentley and Peter Heller, believe a single idea passes through and unifies each stage. For Steiner this idea is the concept of the Ubermensch; for Bentley it is Nietzsche's concept of power; for Heller, it consists of Nietzsche's dedication to the Dionysian process." (Page 352, Vol. 10).

One of the most important results of the re-evaluation of Nietzsche's works over the past 40 years, has been to disassociate him from the Nazis in Germany, who completely falsified his meanings and intentions, and perverted his philosophy of the Ubermensch—the Higher Man in Man—into their precise opposite: military superiority; anti-Semitism and a sick Nationalism. Only by placing the true Nietzsche over against the false picture created by the Nazis, such as was done after 1945 by Kaufman, Heidegger, Camus and others, are we at long last able to see, understand and appreciate the prophetic and timely genius of Nietzsche: a crushed victim of a decadent culture bent on self-destruction; a free spirit martyred on the cross of self-complacent materialism; the courageous fighter for the freedom of the human individual in the world of 'Big Brother'.

* * * * *

In addition to the material contained in this book, Rudolf Steiner often referred to Nietzsche in his various lectures. The following selection from a lecture by Dr. Steiner in Dornach, Switzerland, on March 15, 1924 presents a helpful explanation for some of the seemingly strange events and personal characteristics in Nietzsche's life. This selection also serves as an example of one of the new tools of investigation available to those interested in the laws of human destiny and biography: the Spiritual Scientific Method of Research inaugurated by Rudolf Steiner.

The following copyrighted material is reprinted from the book: *Karmic Relationships: Esoteric Studies*, Volume I, pages 153-158; published by the Anthroposophical Publishing Co., London, 1955.

"I was also intensely interested in the connections of destiny of a man with whom my own life brought me into contact, namely *Friedrich Nietzsche*. I have studied the problem of Nietzsche in all its aspects and, as you know, have written and spoken a great deal about him.

His was indeed a strange and remarkable destiny. I saw him only once during his life. It was in Naumburg, in the nineties of last century, when his mind was already seriously deranged. In the afternoon, about half-past-two, his sister took me into his room. He lay on the couch, listless and unresponsive, with eyes unable to see that someone was standing by him. He lay there with the remarkable, beautifully formed brow that made such a striking impression upon one. Although the eyes were expressionless, one nevertheless had the feeling: This is not a case of insanity, but rather of a man who has been working spiritually the whole morning with great intensity of soul, has had his mid-day meal and is now lying at rest, pondering, half dreamily pondering on what his soul worked out in the morning. Spiritually seen, there were present only a physical body and an etheric body, especially in respect of the upper parts of the organism, for the being of soul-and-spirit was already outside, attached to the body as it were by a stubborn thread only. In reality a kind of death had already set in, but a death that could not be complete because the physical organisation was so healthy. The astral body and the ego that would fain escape were still held by the extraordinarily healthy metabolic and rhythmic organisations, while a completely ruined nerves-and-senses system was no longer able to hold the astral body and the ego. So one had the wonderful impression that the true Nietzsche was hovering above the head. There he was. And down below was something that from the

Foreword

vantage-point of the soul might well have been a corpse, and was only not a corpse because it still held on with might and main to the soul — but only in respect of the lower parts of the organism — because of the extraordinarily healthy metabolic and rhythmic organisation.

Such a spectacle may well make one attentive to the connections of destiny. In this case, at any rate, quite a different light was thrown upon them. Here one could not start from a suffering limb or the like, but one was led to look at the spirituality of Friedrich Nietzsche in its totality.

There are three strongly marked and distinct periods in Nietzsche's life. The first period begins when he wrote *The Birth of Tragedy out of the Spirit of Music* while he was still quite young, inspired by the thought of music springing from Greek tragedy which had itself been born from music. Then, in the same strain, he wrote the four following works: *David Friedrich Strauss: Composer and Author*, *Schopenhauer as Educator*, *Thoughts out of Season*, *Richard Wagner in Bayreuth*. This was in the year 1876. (*The Birth of Tragedy* was written in 1869). *Richard Wagner in Bayreuth* is a hymn of praise to Richard Wagner, actually perhaps the best thing that has been written by any admirer of Wagner.

Then a second period begins. Nietzsche writes his books, *Human, All-too Human*, in two volumes, the work entitled *Dawn* and thirdly, *The Joyful Wisdom*.

In the early writings, up to the year 1876, Nietzsche was in the highest sense of the word an idealist. In the second epoch of his life he bids farewell to idealism in every shape and form; he makes fun of ideals; he convinces himself that if men set themselves ideals, this is due to weakness. When a man can do nothing in life, he says: Life is not worth anything, one must hunt for an ideal. — And so Nietzsche knocks down ideals one by one, puts them to the test, and conceives the manifestations of the Divine in nature as something "all-too-human," something paltry and petty. Here we have Nietzsche the disciple of Voltaire, to whom he dedicates one of his writings. Nietzsche is here the rationalist, the intellectualist. And this phase lasts until about the year 1882 or 1883. Then begins the final epoch of his life, when he unfolds ideas like that of the Eternal Recurrence and presents the figure of Zarathustra as a human ideal. He writes *Thus Spake Zarathustra* in the style of a hymn.

Then he takes out again the notes he had once made on Wagner, and here we find something very remarkable! If one follows Nietzsche's way of working, it does indeed seem strange. Read his work *Richard Wager in Bayreuth.* — It is a grand, enraptured hymn of praise. And now, in the last epoch of his life, comes the book *The Case of Wagner,* in which everything that can possibly be said against Wagner is set down!

If one is content with trivialities, one will simply say: Nietzsche has changed sides, he has altered his views. But those who are really familiar with Nietzsche's manuscripts will not speak in this way. In point of fact, when Nietzsche had written a few pages in the form of a hymn of praise to Wagner, he then proceeded to write down as well everything he could against what he himself had said! Then he wrote another hymn of praise, and then again he wrote in the reverse sense! The whole of *The Case of Wagner* was actually written in 1876, only Nietzsche put it aside, discarded it, and printed only the hymn of praise. And all that he did later on was to take his old drafts and interpolate a few caustic passages.

Foreword

In this last period of his life the urge came to him to carry through an attack which in the first epoch he had abandoned. In all probability, if the manuscript he put aside as being out of keeping with his *Richard Wagner in Bayreuth* had been destroyed by fire, we should never have had *The Case of Wagner* at all.

If you study these three periods in Nietzsche's life you will find that all show evidence of a uniform trend. Even the last book, the last published writing at any rate, *The Twilight of Idols*, which shows entirely his other side — even this last book bears something of the fundamental character of Nietzsche's spiritual life. In old age, however, when this work was composed, he becomes imaginative, writing in a graphic, vividly descriptive style. For example, he wanted to characterise Carlyle, the English writer. He lights on a very apt expression when he speaks of him as having the kind of enthusiasm that takes off its coat. This is a marvellously apt description of one aspect of Carlyle. Other similar utterances — graphic and imaginative — are also to be found in *The Twilight of Idols*.

If you once have this tragic, deeply moving picture before you of the individuality hovering above the body of Nietzsche, you will be compelled to say of his writings that the impression they make is as though Nietzsche were never fully present in his body while he was writing down his sentences. He used to write, you know, sometimes sitting but more often while walking, especially while going for long tramps. It is as though he had always been a little outside his body. You will have this impression most strongly of all in the case of certain passages in the fourth part of *Thus Spake Zarathustra*, of which you will feel that they could have been written only when the body no longer had control, when the soul was outside the body.

One feels that when Nietzsche is being spiritually creative, he always leaves his body behind. And this same tendency can be perceived, too, in his habits. He was particularly fond of taking chloral in order to induce a mood that strives to get away from the body, a mood of aloofness from the body. This tendency was of course due to the fact that the body was in many respects ailing; for example, Nietzsche suffered from constant and always very prolonged headaches, and so on.

All these things give a uniform picture of Nietzsche in this incarnation at the end of the 19th century, an incarnation which finally culminated in insanity, so that he no longer knew who he was. There are letters addressed to George Brandes signed "The Crucified One" — indicating that Nietzsche regards himself as the Crucified One; and at another time he looks at himself as at a man who is actually present outside him, thinks that he is a God walking by the River Po, and signs himself "Dionysos." This separation from the body while spiritual work is going on reveals itself as something that is peculiarly characteristic of this personality, characteristic, that is to say, of this particular incarnation.

If we ponder this inwardly, with Imagination, then we are led back to an incarnation lying not so very long ago. It is characteristic of many such representative personalities that their previous incarnations do not lie in the distant past but in the comparatively near past, even, maybe, quite recent times.

We come to a life where this individuality was a Franciscan, a Franciscan ascetic who inflicted intense self-torture on his body. Now we have the key to the riddle. The gaze falls upon a man in the characteristic Franciscan habit, lying for hours at a time in front of the altar, praying until his knees are bruised and sore, beseeching grace, mortifying his flesh with severest penances — with the result that through the self-inflicted pain he knits himself very strongly with his physical body. Pain makes one intensely aware of the physical body because the astral body yearns after the body that is in pain, wants to penetrate it through and through. The effect of this concentration upon making the body fit for salvation in the one incarnation was that, in the next, the soul had no desire to be in the body at all.

Such are the connections of destiny in certain typical cases. It can certainly be said that they are not what one would have expected! In the matter of successive earthly lives, speculation is impermissible and generally leads to false conclusions. But when we do come upon the truth, marvellous enlightenment is shed upon life.

Because studies of this kind can help us to look at karma in the right way, I have not been afraid — although such a course has its dangers — to give you certain concrete examples of karmic connections which can, I think, throw a great deal of light upon the nature of human karma, of human destiny."

Bernard J. Garber
January 1985

Introduction:

FRIEDRICH NIETZSCHE AND RUDOLF STEINER

AMERICAN READERS have known the writings of Friedrich Nietzsche in English for somewhat less than fifty years. The first translations of Nietzsche's works began appearing in this country shortly after the turn of the century. Since then, almost without interruption American publishers' lists have included collections of his writings, selections from his letters, extracts from his journals, commentaries on his works, and, above all, numerous descriptions of his tragic life story; and American interest in Nietzsche continues today.

In view of this it seems particularly fitting that the present book, with its profound insight into Nietzsche's creative activity, brilliant analysis of his character, and clear evaluation of his significance should be published for the first time in English translation as the second volume of the Centennial Edition of the Major Writings of Rudolf Steiner.

In *Friedrich Nietzsche, Fighter for Freedom*, Rudolf Steiner presents an unforgettable portrait of the man whose writings continue to exercise an important influence in shaping the world in which we live today, and which our children will inherit tomorrow.

*

Friedrich Wilhelm Nietzsche was born in the little village of Röcken near Leipzig on October 15, 1844. As he wrote later, "I was born on the battlefield of Lützen, and the first name I heard was that of Gustavus Adolphus." The Protestant element was in his very blood, for Lutheran clergymen were among his forebearers on both his paternal and maternal sides, while his father was the pastor of Röcken. A tradition that his ancestors were Polish noblemen of the Niëzky family was recorded by Nietzsche himself, as was the statement that his grandmother belonged to the Goethe-Schiller circle of Weimar.

The parsonage life during Nietzsche's early childhood was typical of most of the country clergy-houses of the time. The atmosphere was that of "plain living and high thinking," and the family combined honor and piety with a social life of happiness and cheer, in which a love of music, books and friendships played a role.

When the boy was nearly five, in the summer of 1849, Pastor Nietzsche sustained a severe fall, in consequence of which he died. The widow took her children to Naumberg some months later, and they made their home with the paternal grandparents.

At first Friedrich was enrolled in the municipal school in Naumberg, but shortly afterward he was transferred to a private school in the same town. In October 1858, in

Introduction 13

response to the offer of a scholarship, the boy was enrolled in the Landes-Schule at Pforta. This famous institution had been founded as a Cistercian Abbey in the middle of the twelfth century; at the time of the Reformation it became a secular school. Klopstock, Fichte, Schlegel and Ranke are among the names of those who studied there. In the nineteenth century the Landes-Schule at Pforta was frequently referred to as "the German Eton" because of its excellence in classical studies and as a preparatory school.

Friedrich Nietzsche found a second home in the Landes-Schule; he thoroughly enjoyed his studies—languages, literature and history in particular. In the summer of 1860 he conceived the idea of organizing a literary-artistic club among the students, and this met with a ready response from his schoolmates. Soon the Germania Club, as it came to be called, was organized, and Nietzsche contributed a number of essays on literary and historical themes to the club paper. Many happy hours were spent with his friends at the Germania Club in active discussions about Greek and Latin classics, the works of current German and English authors, and similar subjects. Nietzsche's favorite writers at this time included Emerson, Shakespeare, Tacitus, Aristophanes, Plato and Aeschylus. About *Tristram Shandy* he wrote his sister Elizabeth, "I read it over and over again."

*

While Friedrich Nietzsche was a student at the Landes-Schule, Rudolf Steiner was born on February 27, 1861 in the little town of Kraljevec on the frontier between Hungary and Croatia. His father was a station master in the service of the South Austrian Railway, and the boy's earliest recollections were connected with the activities of the railroad. From his second through his eighth year his impressions were those of the quiet country village of Pottsach, situated in a beautiful green valley at the foot of the magnificent Styrian Alps. The infrequent arrival and departure of the train, the daily activities of the village people, the services at the little church, the colorful peasants and foresters, the life at the local mill, and always and ever the mysterious wonder and beauty of the surrounding nature: all this was a part of the child's world. He attended school in the village for a time; afterward his father undertook to teach him the rudiments of elementary education.

But side by side with this world, the child knew another world, a spiritual world, which was just as real and tangible to him as were the forests, fields and mountains surrounding him. This spiritual world was fiilled with objects and beings, just as the world about him contained stones and plants and animals and people. Even before he was eight, the child could distinguish between these two worlds, and the one was as clear and immediate to him as the other.

Many children have experiences similar to this of Rudolf Steiner. However, generally speaking, with the passing of the years of childhood, these experiences also vanish little by little, until in the retrospect of later years they seem like "the gentle fabric of a dream." But in the instance of Rudolf Steiner, the reality and immediacy of the spiritual world did not fade away; it broadened and deepened into a clear, conscious perception of of beings and events of that world.

In the wondering eyes of this quiet boy there were many questions. He knew, however, that these were questions he could ask of no one around him. More than this, he could speak with no one about the "other" world which was as close and as real to him as were the houses and fields of Pottsach. So he remained silent, and the questions remained alive within him. And, although he shared the daily activities of the children around him, and entered fully into the life of his family, he was unhappy. More than this, he was lonely . . . .

*

In September 1864, Nietzsche left the Landes-Schule with excellent marks, particulary in languages and literature. He entered the University of Bonn a short time later, enrolled as a student of theology and philology. However, he had not been long in the university when his friendship with his professor of philology, Friedrich Wilhelm Ritschel, caused him to drop his theological studies in favor of philology. This action caused great grief to his mother and the other members of his family, who had looked to him to continue the clerical tradition of his father.

A year after he had entered the University of Bonn, Nietzsche withdrew in order to acompany Ritschel, who had been transferred to the faculty of the University of

16   *Friedrich Nietzsche, Fighter for Freedom*

Leipzig. Here he continued his philological studies, and here also two very important events of his life took place. He met Richard Wagner in the home of Professor Brockhaus at Leipzig for the first time; his other meeting happened in a somewhat unusual way.

One day while he was browsing in Rohm's second-hand bookstore in Leipzig, "as if by accident" Nietzsche picked up a copy of Schopenhauer's *Welt als Wille und Vorstellung,* The World as Will and Idea. Without stopping to so much as open the book, he paid for it, and rushed to his lodgings. There he threw himself down on his bed and began to read avidly. As he relates in his journal, "I don't know what daemon told me to take the book home with me. . . . From every line I read I heard a cry of renunciation, denial, resignation. In the book I saw a mirror of the world; life and my own soul were reflected with dreadful faithfulness. The dull, disinterested eye of art looked at me. I saw illness and healing, banishment and restoration, hell and heaven."

Thus, at the age of twenty-one, his reading of Schopenhauer's book—the first part of which had been sold as waste paper shortly after publication because there was no sale for it—changed Nietzsche's outlook upon life. In Shopenhauer he felt he had found his teacher in the fullest, most ideal sense.

After a brief interval spent in military service, during which he sustained a serious chest injury as the result of a fall from a horse, Nietzsche returned to Leipzig to continue his studies in the autumn of 1868. Meanwhile, a series of articles he had contributed to the periodical, the *Rheinisches Museum,* had been read by the authorities of the University of Basel, where a position as professor of classical philology was vacant. A letter was addressed to Ritschel, asking details about Nietzsche, and indicating that the chair at the university might be offered to the young student. Ritschel's reply was unequivocal: "Nietzsche is a genius, and can do whatever he puts his mind to."

This sweeping endorsement must have impressed the authorities at Basel, for they appointed Nietzsche to the post, despite the fact that he had not yet obtained his doctor's degree. One member of the board, however, was slightly dubious of the appointment, for he said, "If the candidate proposed is actually such a genius, perhaps we had better not appoint him, for he would be certain to remain only a short while at such a little university as ours!"

When word of the appointment reached Leipzig, the authorities of the university at once conferred a doctorate upon Nietzsche, without requiring him to undergo further examination. Accordingly, on May 28, 1869, Nietzsche delivered his Innaugural Address at the University of Basel on *Homer and Classical Philology.* He remained in the position for the next ten years, his final retirement being due solely to reasons of health. The foreboding of the official who felt he might "remain only a short while" proved to be ill-founded.

His residence at Basel gave Nietzsche opportunity to follow up his friendship with Richard and Cosima Wagner, and he was often a guest at their Triebschen estate on the Lake of Lucerne, under the shadow of Mount Pilatus.

18   *Friedrich Nietzsche, Fighter for Freedom*

At the same time, he made friends with Jacob Burckhardt, "the hermit-like, secluded thinker," as Nietzsche described him. Burckhardt had recently completed his well-known *Geschichte der Renaissance in Italien*, History of the Renaissance in Italy, 1867, and was famous as the author of a series of critical historical writings on Italian painting, sculpture, and architecture. In addition he occupied the chair of professor of history at the University of Basel.

*

1869 was a year of importance in the life of Rudolf Steiner, now a boy of eight years. Surrounded by the beauties and wonders of nature, puzzling over the intricacies of such mechanical contrivances as the telegraph equipment in the railway station and the machinery in the local mill, the boy's questions moved to a still broader plane. How could he reconcile his direct experience of the spiritual world with the world of sense which surrounded him? Was there a connection between the two? How could one find a bridge between the experiences of the outer and the inner?

The answer came in a most unexpected way.

Among the books of his school teacher in the little Hungarian village of Neudörfl where he now lived with his family, the boy found a textbook on geometry. This volume opened a new world for Rudolf Steiner. In the study of geometry he found answers to his questions. Perhaps even more important, he says, "I learned to know happiness for the first time." His satisfaction was complete, for

Introduction 19

he had discovered that "one can live within the mind in the shaping of forms perceived only within oneself." He had found that an inner joy came to him as he learned through his study of geometry to "lay hold upon something in the spirit alone. . . ."

In the vicinity of his home in Neudörfl was a monastery of the Order of the Most Holy Redeemer. As the boy often met the silent monks on his walks, they aroused solemn feelings in him and he very much wished that they would speak with him. But they never did.

In October, 1870, Rudolf Steiner, now eleven, entered the *Realschule* at Wiener-Neustadt in Austria, traveling backward and forward daily from his home in Neudörfl, which was over the border in Hungary. Along with his intimate contacts with nature which were still an important part of his daily life, the boy now began to find interest in such scientific matters as space and time, attraction and repulsion, atoms and their relation to natural phenomena, and many other subjects. With intense interest his mind turned to science and mathematics, and his teachers in the *Realschule* were of great help to him in these studies.

*

The Franco-Prussian War of 1870 found Nietzsche active as an ambulance attendant in the medical corps, because his health would not permit him to take part in more active combat. However, even these duties proved too much for his strength, and he contracted diphtheria as a result. He returned to his work at the University of

Basel, and in 1872, when he was twenty-eight, Nietzsche published his first major work, the result of his friendship with Wagner and Burkhardt, and the feelings they had evoked in him. This was his *Geburt der Tragödie aus dem Geiste der Musik,* The Birth of Tragedy out of the Spirit of Music. The aesthetic passages attracted musicians to the book, but Nietzsche's colleagues in the philological field greeted it with a bitter attack which was led by Wilamowitz-Moellendorf. The result was that despite efforts on the part of Ritschel and Burckhardt to defend him, Nietzsche had no pupils at all in his philology classes in the winter term of 1872-3.

The aftermath of the German victory in the War of 1870 was the eruption of a nationalistic spirit which had been gathering since the previous successes of 1864 and 1866. Nietzsche felt that this was the time to issue a fiery call to the intellectuals of Germany to abandon what he considered a highly dangerous and unworthy chauvinistic spirit, and to return to their work in the service of true German culture. Richard Wagner joined him in this effort to arouse the German youth to a recognition of the responsibilities their victorious destiny had placed upon them.

Nietzsche devoted parts of his lectures in the university to this subject, and finally, in 1873 he issued the first of a series of pamphlets under the general title, *Unzeitgemässe Betrachtungen,* Thoughts Out of Season, which he called *David Strauss,* dealing with the Philistinism of the period. The second, which was published in the following year, was *Von Nutzen und Nachteil der Historie für das Leben,* The Use and Abuse of History in Life, a sharp attack on the exaggerations of the current "popular historians" of Germany. The third pamphlet was titled, *Schopenhauer als Erzieher,* Schopenhauer as Educator, and appeared in the same year as the second. The last in the series was *Richard Wagner in Bayreuth,* and was published in 1876 when Nietzsche was thirty-two years of age.

Late in August, the first complete performance of Richard Wagner's opera cycle, *Der Ring des Niebelungen* took place in the newly constructed Bayreuth Festival Theatre under the direction of Hans Richter. People flocked to Bayreuth from many countries to attend this cultural event of the first magnitude. Among the spectators was Friedrich Nietzsche who, however, did not share the general enthusiasm for what he saw depicted on the stage.

The well-known French author and critic, Edouard Schuré was also present at the Bayreuth Festival and wrote an account of his meeting with Nietzsche, including a keen appraisal of the latter's character. Schuré's article appeared some years later in the Paris *Revue des Deux Mondes* (1895):

"I met Nietzsche in 1876 when the *Ring of the Niebelungs* had its premiere in Bayreuth. As I spoke with him I was impressed by the high caliber of his mind and by his strange countenance. His forehead was large, his short hair combed well back, and his prominent cheek-bones were those of a Slav. His thick mustache and courageous bearing gave him the look of a cavalry officer, at first glance. However, this was tempered by a certain mixture of arrogance and nervousness difficult to describe.

"The music of his voice and the slowness of his speech expressed his artistic feelings. His circumspect, thoughtful bearing pointed to the philosopher in him. But nothing could have been more misleading than the seeming tranquillity of his expression. The fixed gaze revealed the unhappy task of the thinker; his look combined sharp perception with fanaticism. This double quality made his eye appear uneasy, particularly since it always seemed to be fastened upon a single point. When he spoke for any period of time his face took on the appearance of poetic gentleness, but it was not long before it resumed its antagonistic character.

"When we left (the theatre) together, he spoke no word of censure or disapproval; his face expressed only the sorrowful resignation of a defeated man. . . ."

The year ended badly for Nietzsche. As the months progressed, his health began to fail steadily, and toward the end of the year his symptoms of eye disease were augmented by those of a still graver sort. He withdrew from his university teaching, and was given sick leave.

He passed the winter in Sorrento in company with his friends, Baroness Meysenberg and Dr. Paul Rée, with whom he was to travel considerably in the next years. Despite his illness, he somehow found strength to begin another of his important writings, which would occupy him periodically over the next four years. This was his *Menschliches, Allzumenschliches,* Human, All Too Human.

The three years that followed were a time of increasing illness and loneliness. Finally, Nietzsche resigned his position at the University of Basel in 1879 and was given a retirement pension on which he lived for the rest of his life. The physical and mental suffering he experienced in the year 1879 alone, is described by him: "I have had two hundred days of anguish in this year. . . . My pulse is as slow as that of Napoleon I. . . ."

*

The years between 1873 and '79 were most important in the development of Rudolf Steiner. He then passed his twelfth through eighteenth years. As Nietzsche had discovered Schopenhauer's book in Leipzig, Steiner now saw Kant's *Kritik der reinen Vernunft,* Critique of Pure Reason, in a bookstore window, and eventually came into possession of the volume. From the eager study of this book, to which he devoted every spare moment he could find, often reading single pages "more than twenty times in succession," he hoped to find that which would enable him to understand his own thinking. Yet what he read in Kant was sharply opposed to his own inner conclusion, which he was to describe with the words, "Thinking can be developed to a faculty which really grasps the objects and events of the world."

In this period Steiner deepened his knowledge of mathematics and German literature, in addition to the prescribed courses of study in the *Realschule.* From his fifteenth year onward he spent considerable time tutoring other pupils, thus inaugurating an educational activity that was to accompany him through the coming years. He found that a knowledge of practical psychology was indispensable for this task, and from his experience as a tutor he learned many valuable things about the problems involved in the training of the human mind.

Early in the summer of 1879 Steiner completed his studies at the *Realschule,* and was entered as a student at the *Technische Hochschule* in Vienna for the term to begin in the fall. He spent the summer entirely in the study of philosophy, working his way with utmost care and diligence through the writings of Kant and the principal works of Fichte. He was enrolled for the study of mathematics, natural history, and chemistry.

*

The years from 1879 to 1889 are generally regarded as Nietzsche's time of mature productivity. When one takes into account the suffering he experienced, the restless traveling, his constant loneliness, one is astonished at the amount of creative work he was able to produce during this period. In Italy, the French Riviera, the Swiss Engadine, the urge to write drove him relentlessly.

In July, 1881, his *Morgenröte,* Dawn, was published. Although it received a cold reception, it is of importance, for it marks a turning-point in Nietzesche's creative development. His previous writings had been largely negative and critical in tone. This book marks the appearance of a positive, constructive tendency, which increased in the works which followed.

Although his letters and journals give the impression that the autumn of this year was one of the happiest times of his life, he described the winter as a time "of unbelievable suffering."

Introduction 25

The next summer while Nietzsche was at Tautenberg in Thüringia, Dr. Rée and Baroness Meysenberg introduced him to Miss Andreas Salomé. Out of this and subsequent meetings with Nietzsche, Miss Andreas Salomé later wrote what has been described as "the most unreliable book about Nietzsche which has ever appeared in print."

In July the first performances of Richard Wagner's music drama, *Parsifal*, were given at Bayreuth under the composer's direction. Nietzsche chose this occasion to send Wagner a presentation copy of his *Menschliches, Allzumenschliches*, Human, All Too Human. Curiously enough, at exactly the same time, Wagner sent Nietzsche an inscribed copy of his *Parsifal*. The two packages crossed in the mail. No word of acknowledgment from either recipient was ever forthcoming; the break between Nietzsche and Wagner was complete, although the public was not to become aware of it until six more years had passed. In the meanwhile, Wagner had died suddenly in Venice early in 1883.

The high-point in Nietzsche's creative life came in May, 1883 with the birth of his *Also Sprach Zarathustra,* Thus Spoke Zarathustra, the work which he and many others considered to be his masterpiece. The first part in twenty-three chapters took just ten days to write, as did each of the other parts with the exception of the fourth and last which was completed in 1885. In a letter he said of the writing of his *Zarathustra,* "All of it was conceived in the course of rapid walks . . . absolute certainty, as though each sentence were shouted at one. While writing this book, the greatest physical elasticity and sense of power. . ."

*

Friedrich Nietzsche, Fighter for Freedom

In addition to his studies at the *Technische Hochschule*, Rudolf Steiner attended lectures at the University of Vienna. He particularly appreciated the courses given by the celebrated Karl Julius Schröer on German literature, especially on Schiller and Goethe. As a result, Steiner read Goethe's *Faust* for the first time at the age of nineteen. Later, he enjoyed a personal friendship with Schröer, under whose guidance he came to a deep awareness of the importance of Goethe's contribution to natural science as well as to literature.

Out of his interest in philosophical studies, Steiner attended lectures by the philosophers Robert Zimmerman and Franz Brentano. He studied writings by Ernst Haeckel on morphology, and by Friedrich Theodor Vischer on aesthetics. The writings of Eduard von Hartmann, "the philosopher of the unconscious," interested him deeply, and the day was to come when he would meet this man face to face in Berlin; eventually Steiner would dedicate his book, *Wahrheit und Wissenschaft,* Truth and Science, to him "in warm admiration."

Among the lectures in his scientific courses, those of Edmund Reitlinger on the mechanical theory of heat and on the history of physics made a deep impression on Rudolf Steiner.

At this time Steiner was engaged as tutor in a family where there were four boys, the youngest of whom was a retarded child. The three older boys were no particular problem for him, and their studies went forward without difficulty under his direction. However, the retarded child was a great challenge. That Steiner met this challenge is clear from the fact that in two years the child was able to complete his work in the elementary school and enter the *Gymnasium*. Eventually he entered the School of Medicine and finally graduated as a physician. The experience with this child was reflected in methods for the treatment and care of retarded children which Rudolf Steiner gave some forty years later, thus laying the foundation for a system of Curative Education which is successfully practiced in both Europe and America today.

In 1884 Professor Schröer recommended Steiner to the position of editor and commentator on Goethe's natural scientific writings which the publisher, Joseph Kürschner wished to include in his series of volumes on German literature. In recalling the nature of this task years later, Steiner wrote, "I saw in Goethe a personality who, because of the particular spiritual relation in which he placed man in regard to the world, could also fit the science of nature into the entire realm of human creative activity in the right manner. . . . To me, Goethe was the founder of a science of *organics* . . . applicable to what is alive."

From this time onward, Steiner was occupied with Goethe's investigations in such areas of natural science as metamorphosis, the archetypal plant, the world of animals and minerals, and so on. And out of this study in the light of Goethe's investigations and comments, Steiner came to recognize that if one wishes to understand Goethe as a natural scientist, this can be done only on the basis of learning *how one must perceive* in order to enter into the phenomena of life.

Finally, he realized that no theory of knowledge then

28 *Friedrich Nietzsche, Fighter for Freedom*

extant explained Goethe's particular form of knowledge. Therefore, as a part of his preparatory work before setting about to edit and write commentry on Goethe's natural scientific writings for Kürschner, Steiner drafted a short study of Goethe's theory of knowledge. This was completed in 1886, when Steiner was twenty-five, and is clear proof of his comprehensive grasp of Goethe's way of thinking. The book is titled, *Erkenntnistheorie der Goetheschen Weltanschauung,* Theory of Knowledge in Goethe's Conception of the World, and is one of the most basic of Rudolf Steiner's major writings.

*

In 1886 Nietzsche, now in his forty-second year, wrote his *Jenseits von Gut und Böse,* Beyond Good and Evil, a large part of which was composed during his residence in Italy. This was his first attempt to deal with the subject of the origin of morals. The reaction to the book was generally unfavorable, although Jacob Burckhardt in Basel and Hyppolyte Taine in Paris wrote appreciatively of it.

On July 8th Nietzsche wrote his sister, "My health is actually quite normal, but my soul is very sensitive and is filled with longing for good friends of my own kind. Get me a small circle of men who will listen to me and understand me, and I shall be cured. . . ." No words could better express the poignancy of the pathetic struggle for health and the longing for human beings who "understand."

In 1887 came his *Zur Genealogie der Moral,* The Genealogy of Morals, a further development of the subject which had occupied his mind for some time.

Introduction 29

Finally, in 1888 came the publicizing of his break with Richard Wagner upon the appearance of Neitzsche's book, *Der Fall Wagner,* The Case of Wagner. The volume produced a sensation. It was the first of Nietzsche's works to be reviewed by the public press, and for the first time Nietzsche attracted widespread attention as an author.

Not long before this, Nietzsche had written, "I am the author of fifteen books, and never yet have I seen an honest German review of any of them." Even though this may have been the case, nevertheless Nietzsche had had devoted and entirely capable readers during all his productive years. Among these were Jacob Burckhardt, the Swiss historian, and Hyppolite Taine, the French critic, as we have seen, and also August Strindberg, the Swedish dramatist, and Georg Brandes, the Danish literary historian. It was Brandes who wrote his famous essay about Nietzsche in 1888, thus making his name known in leading intellectual circles throughout Europe. Nietzsche's books began to sell widely. Fame had come at last. . . .

But Nietzsche was fast wearing out; day by day he was fighting against fearful odds. In a pitiful letter to Brandes late in the year, he said, "I have resigned my professorship at the University; I am three parts blind. . . ."

Somehow he managed to complete his *Götzendämmerung,* Twilight of Idols, before the year came to a close.

With the dawn of New Year's Day, 1889, the battle Nietzsche had waged so long was nearly over. For four days he struggled against the gathering shadows, but finally the light of his consciousness flickered out.

On the fourth of January Nietzsche wrote his last letter

in pencil on a scrap of paper torn from a child's notebook. It was addressed to Georg Brandes from Turin: "To the friend Georg: When once you had discovered me, it was easy enough to find me; the difficulty now is to get rid of me." The letter was signed, "The Crucified One."

Nietzsche was forty-five years of age; the long night of spiritual darkness began. . . .

*

While at work on Goethe's natural scientific writings, Steiner was active in the literary and artistic circles of Vienna in the last two years of the eighties. He had many friends among writers, poets, musicians, architects, journalists, scientists and the clergy. Before the Goethe Society of Vienna in 1888 he gave a lecture which reflected his keen interest in the question of artistic beauty. This lecture was subsequently published under the title, *Goethe als Vater einer neuen Ästhetik,* Goethe as Father of a New Aesthetics.

This year was marked by Steiner's first journey into Germany. This was in response to a letter from the administration of the Goethe-Schiller Archives at Weimar inviting him to act as a collaborator on the famous Weimar Edition of Goethe's works then in preparation under commission from the Archduchess Sophie of Saxony. Steiner was well received at Weimar, and from there went to Berlin where he made the acquaintance of Eduard von Hartmann, as we have already seen.

The reading of *Jenseits von Gut und Böse,* Beyond Good and Evil, in 1889 was Steiner's first acquaintance with Nietzsche's writings. He said, "I was fascinated . . . yet repelled at the same time. I found it difficult to discover a right attitude toward Nietzsche. I loved his style, I loved his daring, but I did not love the way he spoke of most significant matters without entering into them in . . . full consciousness. But then I saw that he said many things to which I was very closely related by my own spiritual experience. I felt myself near to his struggle. . . . To me Nietzsche seemed to be one of the most tragic figures of the time.

"I felt that Nietzsche photographed the world from the point to which a deeply significant personality was forced if he had to subsist on the spiritual substance of that time alone, that is, if the vision of the spiritual world did not penetrate into his consciousness. . . .

"This was the picture of Nietzsche that appeared in my thought. It revealed to me the personality who did not see the spirit, but in whom unconsciously the spirit fought against the unspiritual views of the age. . . ."

Steiner's move from Vienna to Weimar was the beginning of a new phase of his life. As a free collaborator in the Goethe-Schiller Archives he could observe events from the vantage point of one of the centers of the cultural life of his time. He came to know many of the leading personalities of the day. He had conversation with men like Hermann Grimm, the art historian and Goethe scholar, Ernst Haeckel, the scientist and German interpreter of Darwin, Ludwig Laistner, author and literary advisor to the internationally-known Cotta publishing firm, and many others. Laistner invited Steiner to edit editions of

32   *Friedrich Nietzsche, Fighter for Freedom*

Schopenhauer and Jean Paul Richter, which were published by Cotta in their *Library of World Literature*. Steiner fulfilled this task, including writing introductions to the writings of both authors.

In 1891 Steiner received his Ph.D. at the University of Rostock. His thesis dealt with the scientific teaching of Fichte. In somewhat enlarged form this thesis appeared under the title *Wahrheit und Wissenschaft*, Truth and Knowledge, as the preface to Steiner's chief philosophical work, *Die Philosophie der Freiheit*, The Philosophy of Spiritual Activity, 1894.

And now events occurred which finally brought Rudolf Steiner into the company of those around Nietzsche, who was being cared for at the home of his mother in Naumberg.

In his autobiography Steiner describes a significant meeting: "One day Nietzsche's sister, Elizabeth Foerster-Nietzsche, visited the Goethe-Schiller Archives. She was about to take the first step toward forming the Nietzsche Archives, and wanted to know how the Goethe-Schiller Archives were managed. A short time afterward the publisher of Nietzsche's works, Fritz Koegel, also appeared in Weimar, and I came to know him. . . .

"I am thankful to Frau Foerster-Nietzsche that during the first of my many visits (to Nietzsche's home), she led me into the room of Friedrich Nietzsche. There on a couch he lay in spirit-night, with his marvelously beautiful brow, that of artist and thinker in one. It was early in the afternoon. Those eyes, which even in thir dimness gave the effect of soul penetration, still took in a picture of the

Introduction 33

surrounding, but this had no entrance into the soul. One stood there and Nietzsche was unaware of it. And yet one could have believed that this spiritually illuminated countenance expressed a soul which had formed thoughts within itself all morning, and now wished to rest for a while. A deep inner shudder which seized my soul . . . transformed itself into an understanding for the genius whose look was directed toward me, but which did not meet mine. . . .

"And before my soul stood the soul of Nietzsche, as if floating above his head, already boundless in its spirit light, freely surrendered to the spirit world, for which it had longed before this darkened condition, but did not find. . . .

"Previously I had *read* the Nietzsche who had written; now I *saw* the Nietzsche who, from far distant spirit fields carried within his body ideas which still shimmered in beauty, despite the fact that on the way they had lost their original power of light. I saw a soul which had brought rich gold of enlightenment from earlier earth lives, but which it could not bring to full radiance in this life. I had admired what Nietzsche had written, but now behind my admiration I glimpsed a radiant picture.

"In my thoughts I could only stammer about what I had seen, and that stammering is the content of my book. . . . It was the picture of Nietzsche which had inspired it.

"Frau Foerster-Nietzsche had asked that I arrange the Nietzsche library. Thus I was permitted to spend several weeks in the Nietzsche Archives in Naumberg. It was a beautiful task that brought before me books that Nietzsche had read. His spirit lived in the impressions these volumes made. . . . A book by Emerson, covered with marginal notes, bore traces of the most devoted, intense study. . . .

"My relationship with the Nietzsche Archives was a very stimulating episode in my life in Weimar. . . ."

*

In 1897 Nietzsche's mother died, and his sister took him into her home, where he passed his last years. In this same year Rudolf Steiner wrote his *Goethes Weltanschauung*, Goethe's Conception of the World, a rich harvest from his work in Vienna and Weimar in close study of Goethe's contribution to the knowledge of man and nature. This book marked the end of Steiner's residence in Weimar, for he now moved to Berlin to assume the editorship of *Das Magazin für Litteratur*, a well-known literary periodical which had been founded by Joseph Lehmann in 1832.

*

On the twenty-fifth of August, 1900, Friedrich Nietzsche died. He was buried in the graveyard at Röcken near the church where his father had preached, and the parsonage where he had been born fifty-six years before.

In Berlin, two weeks after Friedrich Nietzsche's death, Rudolf Steiner gave a Memorial Address in his honor, the text of which is included in the present volume.

*

In his *Fors Clavigera,* John Ruskin wrote, "Youth is properly a forming time—that in which a man makes himself, or is made, what he is to be. Then comes the time of labor, when, having become the best he can be, he does the best he can do. Then the time of death, which, in happy lives, is very short; but always a *time*. The ceasing to breathe is only the *end* of death."

For the Fighter for Freedom, the end of death had come at last.

PAUL MARSHALL ALLEN

Englewood, New Jersey
February, 1960

PART ONE

FRIEDRICH NIETZSCHE
A FIGHTER AGAINST HIS TIME

PREFACE TO THE FIRST EDITION (1895)

WHEN I BECAME acquainted with the works of Friedrich Nietzsche six years ago, ideas had already formed within me which were similar to his. Independently, and from completely different directions, I came to concepts which were in harmony with those Nietzsche expressed in his writings: *Zarathustra, Jenseits von Gut and Böse,* Beyond Good and Evil, *Genealogie der Moral,* Genealogy of Morals, and *Götzendämmerung,* Twilight of Idols. In my little book which appeared in 1886, *Erkenntnistheorie der Goetheschen Weltanschauung,* The Theory of Knowledge in Goethe's World Conception, this same way of implicit thinking is expressed as one finds in the works of Nietzsche mentioned above.

This is why I feel myself impelled to draw a picture of Nietzsche's life of reflection and feeling. I believe that such a picture will be most like Nietzsche when it is created according to his last writings. This I have done. The earlier writings of Nietzsche show him as *a searcher*. He presents himself to us as a restless striver toward the heights. In his last writings we see him when he has reached the summit, and at a height commensurate with his very own spiritual quality. In most of the writings which have appeared about Nietzsche up to now, this development is represented as if in the various periods of his writing he had more or less contradictory opinions. I have tried to show that there is no question of a change of opinion in Nietzsche, but rather of a movement upward, of a development of a personality in a manner fitting to it, which had not yet found a form of expression in accord with his innate points of view in those first works.

The final goal of Nietzsche's creativity is the description of the "superman." I considered my chief task in this writing to be the characterization of this type. My characterization of the superman is exactly the opposite of the caricature developed in the currently popular book about Nietzsche by Frau Lou Andreas Salomé. One cannot put into the world anything more contrary to Nietzsche's spirit than the mystical monster she has made out of the superman. My book shows that in Nietzsche's ideas nowhere is the least trace of mysticism to be found. I did not allow myself to be drawn into the refutation of Frau Salomé's opinion that Nietzsche's thoughts in *Menschliches, Allzumenschliches,* Human, All Too Human, were influenced by the works of Paul Rée, the editor of *Psychological Observations* and *The Origin of Moral Feelings,* etc. Such an average brain as that of Paul Rée could make no important impression on Nietzsche. Even now I would not touch upon these things at all if the book of Frau Salomé had not contributed so much toward the spreading of downright disagreeable judgments about

Preface

Nietzsche. Fritz Koegel, the excellent publisher of Nietzsche's works, bestowed upon this bungled piece of work its deserved treatment in the *Magazine for Literature*.

I cannot conclude this short preface without giving hearty thanks to Nietzsche's sister, Frau Foerster-Nietzsche, for the many friendly deeds I experienced from her during the period in which this book developed. I owe to her the hours spent in the Nietzsche Archives, and the mood out of which the following thoughts were written.

RUDOLF STEINER

Weimar, April, 1895.

i THE CHARACTER

1.

FRIEDRICH NIETZSCHE characterizes himself as a *lonely* ponderer and friend of riddles, as a personality *not made for the age in which he lived*. The one who follows such paths as his, "meets no one; this is a part of going one's own way. No one approaches to help him; all that happens to him of danger, accidents, evil and bad weather, he must get along with alone," he says in the preface of the second edition of his *Morgenröte,* Dawn. But it is stimulating to follow him into his loneliness. In the words in which he expressed his relationship to Schopenhauer, I would like to describe my relationship to Nietzsche: "I belong to those readers of Nietzsche who, after they have read the first page, know with certainty that they will read all pages, and listen to every word he has said. My confidence in him was there immediately . . . I understood him as if he had written just for me, in order to express all that I would say intelligibly but immediately and foolishly." One can speak thus and yet be far from acknowledging oneself as a "believer" in Nietzsche's world conception. But Nietzsche himself could not be further from wishing to have

The Character 43

such "believers." Did he not put into Zarathustra's mouth these words:

"You say you believe in Zarathustra, but of what account is Zarathustra? You are my believer, but of what account are all believers?

"You have not searched for yourselves as yet; there you found me. Thus do all believers, but, for that reason, there is so little in all believing.

"Now I advise you to forsake me and to find *yourselves;* and only when all of you have denied me will I return to you."

Nietzsche is no Messianic founder of a religion; therefore he can wish for friends who support his opinion, but he cannot wish for confessors to his teaching, who give up their own selves to find his.

In Nietzsche's personality are found instincts which are contrary to the complete gamut of the ideas of his contemporaries. With instinctive aversion he rejects most of the important cultural ideas of those amid whom he developed himself and, indeed, not as one rejects an assertion in which one has discovered a logical contradiction, but rather as one turns away from a color which causes pain to the eye. The aversion starts from the immediate feeling; to begin with, conscious thinking does not come into consideration at all. What other people feel when such thoughts as guilt, conscience, sin, life beyond, ideal happiness, fatherland, pass through their heads, works unpleasantly upon Nietzsche. The instinctive manner of rejection of these ideas also differentiates Nietzsche from the so-called "free thinkers" of the present. The latter know all the intellectual objections to "the old illusionary ideas," but how rarely is one found who can say that his *instincts* no longer depend upon them! It is precisely the instincts which play bad tricks upon the free thinkers of the present time. The thinking takes on a character independent of the inherited ideas, but the instincts cannot adapt themselves to the changed character of the intellect. These "free thinkers" put just any belief of modern science in place of an old idea, but they speak about it in such a way that one realizes that the intellect goes another way from that of the instincts. The intellect searches in *matter,* in *power,* in the *laws of nature,* for the origin of phenomena; but the instincts misguide so that one has the same feeling toward this being that others have toward their personal God. Intellects of this type defend themselves against the accusation of the denial of God, but they do not do this because their world conception leads them to something which is in harmony with any form of God, but rather because from their forefathers they have inherited the tendency to feel an *instinctive* shudder at the expression, "the denial of God." Great natural scientists emphasize that they do not wish to banish such ideas as God and immortality, but rather that they wish to transform them, in the sense of modern science. Their instincts simply have remained behind their intellect.

A large number of these "free spirits" are of the opinion that the will of man is unfree. They say that under certain circumstances man *must* behave as his character and the conditions working upon him force him to act. But if we look at the opponents of the theory of "free will," we shall find that the instincts of these "free spirits" turn away from a doer of an "evil" deed with exactly the same aversion as do the instincts of those who represent the opinion that according to its desires the "free will" could turn itself toward good or toward evil.

The contradiction between intellect and instinct is the mark of our "modern spirits." Within the most liberal thinkers of the present age the implanted instincts of Christian orthodoxy also still live. Exactly opposite instincts are active in Nietzsche's nature. He does not need first to reflect whether there are reasons against the acceptance of a personal world leader. His instinct is too proud to bow before such an one; for this reason he rejects such a representation. He says in his *Zarathustra,* "But that I may reveal to you my heart, to you, my friends: *if* there were Gods, how could I stand it not to be a God! *Therefore,* there are no Gods." Nothing in his inner being compels him to accuse either himself or another as "guilty" of a committed action. To consider such a "guilty" action as unseemly, he needs no theory of "free" or "unfree" will.

The patriotic feelings of his German compatriots are also repugnant to Nietzsche's instincts. He cannot make his feelings and his thinking dependent upon the circles of the people amid whom he was born and reared, nor upon the age in which he lives. "It is so small-townish," he says in his *Schopenhauer als Erzieher,* Schopenhauer as Educator, "to make oneself duty-bound to opinions which no longer bind one a few hundred miles away. Orient and Occident are strokes of chalk which someone draws before our eyes to make fools of our timidity. I will make the attempt to come to freedom, says the young soul to itself; and then should it be hindered because accidentally two nations hate and fight each other, or because an ocean lies between two parts of the earth, or because there a religion is taught which did not exist a few thousand years previously?" The soul experiences of the Germans during the War of 1870 found so little echo in his soul that "while the thunder of battle passed from Wörth over Europe," he sat in a small corner of the Alps, "brooding and puzzled, consequently most grieved, and at the same time not grieved," and wrote down his thoughts about the Greeks. And, a few weeks later, as he found himself "under the walls of Metz," he still was not freed from the questions which he had concerning the life and art of the Greeks. (See *Versuch einer Selbstkritik*, Attempt at a Self-Critique, in the 2nd edition of his *Geburt der Tragödie*, Birth of Tragedy.) When the war came to an end, he entered so little into the enthusiasm of his German contempories over the decisive victory that in the year 1873 in his writing about David Strauss he spoke about "the bad and dangerous consequences" of the victorious struggle. He even represented it as insanity that German culture should have been victorious in this struggle, and he described this insanity as dangerous because if it should become dominant within the German nation, the danger would exist of transforming the victory into complete defeat; a defeat, yes, an extirpation of the German spirit in favor of "the German realm." This was Nietzsche's attitude at a time when the whole of Europe was filled with national fanaticism. It is the thinking of a personality *not in harmony*

The Character

with his time, of a fighter against his time. Much more could be added to what has been said to show that Nietzsche's life of feeling and reflection was completely different from that of his contemporaries.

2.

Nietzsche is no "thinker" in the usual sense of the word. For the deeply penetrating and valid questions which he had to ask in regard to the world and life, mere thinking was not sufficient. For these questions, all the forces of human nature must be unchained; *intellectual* thinking alone is not sufficient for the task. Nietzsche has no confidence in *merely intellectually conceived* reasons for an opinion. "There is a mistrust in me for dialectic, even for proofs" he writes to Georg Brandes on the 2nd of December, 1887 (see his *Menschen und Werke*, Men and Works, p. 212). For those who would ask the reasons for his opinions, he is ready with the answer of Zarathustra, "You ask why? I do not belong to those of whom one may ask their why." For him, a criterion was not that an opinion could be proved logically, but rather if it acted upon all forces of the human personality in such a way that it had *value for life*. He grants validity to a thought only if he finds it will add to the development of life. To see man as healthy as possible, as powerful as possible, as creative as possible, is his desire. Truth, beauty, all ideals, have value and concern the human being only to the extent that they *foster life*.

The question about the *value of truth* appears in several of Nietzsche's writings. In the most daring form it is asked in his *Jenseits von Gut und Böse,* Beyond Good and Evil. "The will for truth which has misled us into so many hazards, that famous truthfulness, about which all philosophers have spoken with awe: what questions this will for truth has already put before us! What marvelous, difficult, worthy questions! This is already a long story, yet it seems that it has barely begun. Is it any wonder that we finally become mistrustful, lose patience, turn about impatiently? Is it any wonder that from the Sphinx we ourselves also learn to ask questions? Then who is it who asks questions here? What is it in us that really wants to penetrate 'to truth?' In fact, we had to stand for a long time before the question about the cause of will—until we finally remained completely still before a yet more fundamental question. We asked about *the value of willing.* That is, provided we want truth; *why not rather untruth?"*

This is a thought of a boldness hardly to be surpassed. If one places beside it what another daring "ponderer and friend of riddles," Johann Gottlieb Fichte, said about the striving after truth, then one realizes for the first time from what depths of human nature Nietzsche brings forth his ideas. "I am destined," said Fichte, "to bear witness to truth; upon my life and my destiny, nothing depends; upon the effects of my life, infinitely much depends. I am a priest of truth; I am in its debt; for it I have bound myself to do all, to dare all, and to suffer all." (Fichte, *Über die Bestimmung des Gelehrten,* On the Task of the Scholar, Lecture 4). These words describe the relationship of the most noble spirits of the newer Western culture to truth. In the face of all of Nietzsche's cited ex-

The Character

pressions, they appear superficial. Against them one can ask, Is it not possible that untruth has more valuable effects upon life than truth? Is it impossible that truth harms life? Has Fichte himself posed these questions? Have others done it who have borne "witness to truth?"

But Nietzsche poses these questions. And he believes that he can become clear only when he treats this striving after truth not merely as an intellectual matter, but seeks the instincts which bring forth this striving. For it could well have been that these instincts make use of truth only as a medium to accomplish something which stands higher than truth. Nietzsche thinks after he has "looked at the philosophers long enough between the lines and upon the fingers," that "most thinking of philosophers is secretly led by their instincts, and forced along definite ways." The philosophers consider that the final impulse to action is the striving after truth. They believe this because they are unable to look into the depths of human nature. In reality, this striving after truth is guided by the *will to power*. With the help of truth, this power and fullness of life should be increased for the personality. The conscious thinking of the philosopher is of the opinion that the recognition of truth is a final goal; the unconsicous instinct that motivates this thinking strives toward the fostering of life. From this instinct, "the falsity of a judgment is no real objection toward a judgment;" for him only the question comes into consideration, "to what extent is it life furthering, life supporting, species supporting, perhaps even species cultivating." (*Jenseits von Gut und Böse,* Beyond Good and Evil, ¶ 4.)

"Do you call will to truth, you wisest ones, that which impels you and makes you ardent?"

"Will for the conceivableness of all being: thus do *I* name your will!

"All being would you first *make* conceivable, because you doubt with good reason whether it is already thinkable.

"But it shall yield to you and bend itself to you! So wills your will. Smooth shall it become, and subject to the spirit, as its mirror and reflection.

"That is your entire will, you wisest ones, a *Will to Power.*" (*Zarathustra*, second part, *The Self Surpassing.*)

Truth is to make the world subservient to the spirit, and thereby serve life. Only as a life necessity has it value. But can one not go further and ask, What is this life worth in itself? Nietzsche considers such a question to be impossible. That everything alive wants to live as powerfully, as meaningfully as possible, he accepts as a fact about which he ponders no further. Life instincts ask no further about the value of life. They ask only what possibilities there are to increase the strength of its bearers. "Judgments, evaluations of life, either for or against, can never be true, in the final analysis; they have value only as symptoms, they come into consideration only as symptoms, and in themselves such judgments are nonsense. One must absolutely stretch out one's fingers and try to comprehend the astonishing finesse in the fact that *the value of life cannot be measured.* It cannot be measured by a living person because he partakes of it; indeed, for him it is even an object of strife: therefore he is no judge; neither can it be appraised by a dead person, for another reason. For a philosopher to see a problem in the value of life remains, so to speak, an accusation against him, a question concerning his wisdom and lack of wisdom." (*Götzendämmerung, Das Problem des Sokrates,* The Twilight of Idols, The Problem of Socrates.) The question about the value of life exists only for a poorly educated, sick personality. A well-rounded personality *lives* without asking how much his life is worth.

Because Nietzsche has the point of view described above, he places such little weight upon logical proofs for a judgment. It is of little account to him that a judgment lets itself be proved logically; he is interested in whether one can live well under its influence. Not alone the intellect, but the whole personality of the human being must be satisfied. The best thoughts are those which bring all forces of human nature into an activity adapted to the person.

Only thoughts of this nature have interest for Nietzsche. He is not a philosophical brain, but a "gatherer of honey of the intellect" who searches for "honey baskets" of knowledge, and tries to bring home what benefits life.

3.

In Nietzsche's personality, those instincts rule which make man a dominating, controlling being. Everything pleases him which manifests might; everything displeases him which discloses weakness. He feels happy only so long as he finds himself in conditions of life which heighten his power. He loves hindrances, obstacles against his activity, because he becomes aware of his own power by overcoming them. He looks for the most difficult paths which the human being can take. A fundamental trait of his character is expressed in the verse which he has written on the title page of the second edition of his *Fröhliche Wissenschaft,* Joyful Wisdom:

> "I live in my own house,
> Have never copied anything from anyone,
> And have ridiculed every master
> Who has not ridiculed himself."

Every kind of subordination to a strange power Nietzsche feels as weakness. And he thinks differently about that which is a "strange power" than many a one who considers himself to be "an independent, free spirit." Nietzsche considers it a weakness when the human being subordinates his thinking and his doing to so-called "eternal, brazen" laws of the intellect. Whatever the uniformly developed personality does, it does not allow it to be prescribed by a moral science, but only by the impulses of its own self. Man is already weak at the moment he *searches* for laws and rules according to which he *shall* think and act. Out of his own being the strong individual *controls* his way of thinking and doing.

Nietzsche expresses this opinion in the crudest form in sentences, because of which narrow-minded people have characterized him as a downright dangerous spirit: "When the Christian Crusaders in the East came into collision with that invincible order of assassins, those orders of free thinking spirits, *par excellence,* whose lowest order lived in a state of discipline such as no order of monks ever at-

The Character

tained, in some way or other they managed to get an inkling of that symbol and motto that was reserved for the highest grade alone, as their secret: '*Nothing is true, everything is permissible!*' ... Truly, that was *freedom* of the spirit; thereby faith itself was giving notice to truth." (*Genealogie der Moral,* Genealogy of Morals, 3rd Section, ¶ 24.) That these sentences are the expression of feelings of an aristocratic, of a master nature, which will not permit the individual to live freely according to his *own* laws, with no regard to the eternal truths and rules of morality, those people do not feel who by nature are adjusted to subordination. A personality such as Nietzsche cannot bear those tyrants who appear in the form of abstract moral commandments. *I* determine how I am to think, how I am to act, says such a nature.

There are people who base their justification for calling themselves "free thinkers" upon the fact that in their thinking and acting they do not subject themselves to those laws which are derived from other human beings, but only to "the eternal laws of the intellect," the "incontrovertible concepts of duty," or "the Will of God." Nietzsche does not regard such people as really *strong* personalities. For they do not think and act according to their own nature, but according to the *commands* of a higher authority. Whether the slave follows the arbitrariness of his master, the religious the revealed verities of a God, or the philosopher the demands of the intellect, this changes nothing of the fact that they are all *obeyers*. What does the commanding is of no importance; the deciding factor is that there is *commanding,* that the human being does not give his own direction for his acting, but thinks that there is a power which delineates this direction.

The strong, truly free human being will not *receive* truth, he will *create* it; he will not let something "be permitted" him; he will not obey. "The real philosophers are *commanders* and *law givers;* they say, '*Thus shall it be*,' they first decide the 'why' and 'wherefore' and thereby dispose of the preliminary labor of all philosophical workers, all conquerors of the past; they grasp at the future with creative hands and all that is and was becomes for them a means, a tool, a hammer. Their 'knowing' is *creating,* their creating is a law-giving, their will to truth is *Will to Power*. Are there such philosophers today? Were there once such philosophers? *Must* there not be such philosophers?" (*Jenseits von Gut und Böse,* Beyond Good and Evil, ¶ 211.)

4.

Nietzsche sees a special indication of human weakness in every type of belief in a world beyond, in a world other than that in which man lives. According to him, one can do no greater harm to life than to order one's existence in this world according to another life in a world beyond. One cannot give oneself over to greater confusion than when one assumes the existence of beings behind the phenomena of this world, beings which are not approachable by human knowledge, and which are to be considered as the real basis, as the decisive factor in all existence. By such an assumption one ruins for oneself the joy in this world. One degrades it to illusion, to a mere reflection of

The Character 55

the inaccessible. One interprets the world known to us, the world which for us is the only real one, as a futile dream, and attributes true reality to an imaginery, fictitious other world. One interprets the human senses as deceivers, who give us only illusory pictures instead of realities.

Such a point of view cannot stem from weakness. For the strong person who is deeply rooted in reality, who has joy in life, will not let it enter his head to imagine another reality. He is occupied with this world and needs no other. But the suffering, the ill, those dissatisfied with this life, take refuge in the yonder. What this life has taken away from them, the world beyond is to offer them. The strong, healthy person who has well developed senses fitted to search for the causes of this world in this world itself, requires no causes or beings of the world beyond for the understanding of the appearances within which he lives. The weak person, who perceives reality with crippled eyes and ears, needs causes behind the appearances.

Out of suffering and sick longing, the belief in the yonder world is born. Out of the inability to penetrate the real world all acceptances of "things in themselves" have originated.

All who have reason to deny the *real* life say *Yes* to an *imaginary* one. Nietzsche wants to be an *affirmer* in face of reality. He will explore this world in all directions; he will penetrate into the depths of existence; of another life he wants to know nothing. Even suffering itself cannot provoke *him* to say No to life, for suffering also is a means to knowledge. "Like a traveler who plans to awaken at a certain hour, and then peacefully succumbs to sleep, we philosophers surrender ourselves to sickness, provided that we have become ill for a time in body and soul; we also close our eyes. And as the traveler knows that somewhere something does *not* sleep, that something counts the hours and will awaken him, so we also know that the decisive moment will find us awake—that then something will spring forth and catch the spirit *in the act;* I mean, in the weakness or the turning back or the surrendering or the hardening or the beclouding, as all the many sick conditions of the spirit are called, which in days of health had the *pride* of spirit against them. After such a self-questioning, self-examination, one learns to look with a finer eye at everything which had been philosophized about until now." (Preface to the second edition of *Fröhliche Wissenschaft,* Joyful Wisdom.)

5.

Nietzsche's friendly attitude toward life and reality shows itself also in his point of view in regard to men and their relationships with each other. In this field Nietzsche is a complete individualist. Each human being is for him a world in itself, a *unicum.* "This marvelously colorful manifoldness which is unified to a 'oneness' and faces us as a certain human being, no accident, however strange, could shake together in a like way a second time." (*Schopenhauer als Erzieher,* Schopenhauer as Educator, ¶ 1.) Very few human beings, however, are inclined to unfold their individualities, which exist but once. They are in terror of the loneliness into which they are forced because of this. It is more comfortable and less dangerous to live

The Character 57

in the same way as one's fellow men; there one always finds company. The one who arranges his life in his own way is not understood by others, and finds no companions. Loneliness has a special attraction for Nietzsche. He loves to search for secrets within his own self. He flees from the community of human beings. For the most part, his ways of thought are attempts to search for treasures which lie deeply hidden within his personality. The light which others offer him, he despises; the air one breathes where the "community of human beings," the "average man" lives, he will not breathe. Instinctively he strives toward his "citadel and privacy" where he is *free* from the crowds, from the many, from the majority. (*Jenseits von Gut und Böse,* Beyond Good and Evil, ¶ 26). In his *Fröliche Wissenschaft,* Joyful Wisdom, he complains that it is difficult for him to "digest" his fellow men; and in *Jenseits von Gut und Böse,* Beyond Good and Evil, ¶ 282, he discloses that at the least he carried away dangerous intestinal disturbances when he sat down at the table where the diet of "ordinary human beings" was served. Human beings must not come too close to Nietzsche if he is to stand them.

6.

Nietzsche grants validity to a thought, a judgment, in the form to which the free-reigning life instincts give their assent. Attitudes which are decided by life he does not allow to be removed by logical doubt. For this reason his thinking has a firm, free swing. It is not confused by reflections as to whether an assumption is also true "objectively," whether it does not go beyond the boundaries of the possibilities of human knowledge, etc. When Nietzsche has recognized the value of a judgment for life, he no longer asks for a further "objective" meaning and validity. And he does not worry about the limits of knowledge. It is his opinion that a healthy thinking creates what it is able to create, and does not torment itself with the useless question, What can I *not* do?

The one who wishes to determine the value of a judgment by the degree to which it furthers life, can, of course, only do this on the basis of his own personal life impulses and instincts. He can never wish to say more than, Insofar as my own life instincts are concerned, I consider this particular judgment to be valuable. And Nietzsche never wishes to say anything else when he expresses a point of view. It is just this relationship of his to his thought world which works so beneficially upon the reader who is orientated toward freedom. It gives Nietzsche's writings a character of unselfish, modest dignity. In comparison, how repellent and immodest it sounds when other thinkers believe their person to be the organ by which eternal, irrefutable verities are made known to the world. One can find sentences in Nietzsche's works which express his strong ego-consciousness, for example, "I have given to mankind the deepest book which it possesses, my *Zarathustra;* soon I shall give it the most independent." (*Götzendämmerung*, Twilight of Idols, ¶ 51.) But what do these words indicate? I have dared to write a book whose content is drawn from lower depths of a personality than is usual in similar books, and I shall offer a book which is more independent of every strange judgment than other

The Character

philosophical writings, for I shall speak about the most important things only in the way they relate to my personal instincts. That is dignified modesty. It would of course go against the taste of those whose lying humility says, I am nothing, my work is everything; I bring nothing of my personal feelings into my books, but I express only what the pure intellect allows me to express. Such people want to deny their person in order to assert that their expressions are those of a higher spirit. Nietzsche considers his thoughts to be the results of his own person and nothing more.

7.

The specialist philosophers may smile about Nietzsche, or give us their impressions about the "dangers" of his "world conception" as best they can. Of course, many of these spirits, who are nothing but animated textbooks of logic, are not able to praise Nietzsche's creations, which spring from the most mighty, most immediate life impulses.

In any case, with his bold thought Nietzsche leaps and hits upon deeper secrets of human nature than many a logical thinker with his cautious creeping. Of what use is all logic if it catches only worthless content in its net of concepts? When valuable thoughts are communicated to us, we rejoice in them alone, even if they are not tied together with logical threads. The salvation of life does not depend upon logic alone, but also upon the production of thoughts. At present our specialized philosophy is sufficiently unproductive, and it could very well use the stimulation of the thoughts of a courageous, bold writer like Nietzsche. The power of development of their specialized philosophy is paralyzed through the influence which the thinking of Kant has made upon them. Through this influence it has lost all originality, all courage. From the academic philosophy of his time Kant has taken over the concept of truth which originates from "pure reason." He has tried to show that through such truth we cannot learn to know things which lie beyond our experience of "things in themselves." During the last century, infinite, immeasurable cleverness was expended to pentrate into these thoughts of Kant's from all directions. The results of this sharp thinking are unfortunately rather meager and trivial. Should one translate the banalities of many a current philosophical book from academic formulae into healthy speech, such content would compare rather poorly with many a short aphorism of Nietzsche's. In view of present-day philosophy, the latter could speak the proud sentence with a certain justice, "It is my ambition to say in ten sentences what others say in one book—what every other person does *not* say in one book. . . ."

8.

As Nietzsche does not want to express anything but the results of his personal instincts and impulses, so to him strange points of view are nothing more than symptoms from which he draws conclusions about the ruling instincts of individual human beings or whole peoples, races, and so on. He does not occupy himself with discussions or arguments over strange opinions. But he looks for the instincts

The Character

which are expressed in these opinions. He tries to discover the character of the personalities or people from their attitudes. Whether an attitude indicates the dominance of instincts for health, courage, dignity, joy, and life, or whether it originates from unhealthy, slavish, tired instincts, inimical to life, all this interests him. Truths in themselves are indifferent to him; he concerns himself with the way people develop their truths according to their instincts, and how they further their life goals through them. He looks for the natural causes of human attitudes.

Nietzsche's striving, of course, is not according to the tendencies of those idealists who attribute an independent value to truth, who want to give it "a purer, higher origin" than that of the instincts. He explains human views as the result of natural forces, just as the natural scientist explains the structure of the eye from the cooperation of natural causes. He recognizes an explanation of the spiritual development of mankind out of special moral purposes, or ideals out of a moral world order, as little as the natural scientist of today recognizes the explanation that nature has built the eye in a certain way for the reason that nature had the *intention* to create an organ of seeing for the organism. In every ideal Nietzsche sees only the expression of an instinct which looks toward satisfaction in a definite form, just as the modern natural scientist sees in the intentional arrangement of an organ, the result of organic formative laws. If at present there still exist natural scientists and philosophers who reject all purposeful creating in nature, but who stop short before moral idealism, and see in history the realization of a divine will, an ideal order of things, this belief is an incompleteness of the instinct. Such people lack the necessary perspective for the judging of spiritual happenings, while they have it for the observation of natural happenings. When a human being thinks he is striving toward an ideal which does not derive from reality, he thinks this only because he does not recognize the instinct from which this ideal stems.

Nietzsche is an anti-idealist in that sense in which the modern natural scientist opposes the assumption of purposes which nature is to materialize. He speaks just as little about moral purposes as the natural scientist speaks about natural purposes. Nietzsche does not consider it wiser to say, Man should materialize a moral ideal, than to explain that the bull has horns so that he may gore with them. He considers the one as well as the other expression to be a product of a world explanation which speaks about "divine providence," " wise omnipotence," instead of natural causes.

This world clarification is a check to all sound thinking; it produces a fictitious fog of ideals which prevents that natural power of seeing, orientated to the observation of reality, that ability to fathom world events; finally, it completely dulls all sense for reality.

9.

When Nietzsche engages in a spiritual battle he doesn't wish to contradict foreign opinions as such, but he does so because these opinions point to instincts harmful and contrary to nature, against which he wishes to fight. In this regard his intention is similar to that of someone who attacks a harmful natural phenomenon or destroys a dangerous creature. He does not count on the "convincing" power of truth, but on the fact that he will conquer his opponent because the latter has unsound, harmful instincts, while he himself has sound, life-furthering instincts. He looks for no further justification for such a battle when his instinct considers his opponent to be harmful. He does not believe that he has to fight as the representative of an idea, but he fights because his instincts compel him to do so. Of course, it is the same with any spiritual battle, but ordinarily the fighters are as little aware of the real motivations as are the philosophers of their "Will to Power," or the followers of a moral world order of the natural causes of their moral ideals. They believe that only opinions fight opinions, and they disguise their true motives by cloaks of concepts. They also do not mention the instincts of the opponents which are unsympathetic to them; indeed, perhaps these do not enter their consciousness at all. In short, these forces which are really hostile toward each other do not come out into the open at all. Nietzsche mentions unreservedly those instincts of his opponents which are disagreeable to him, and he also mentions the instincts with which he opposes them. One who wishes to call this *cynicism* may well do so. But he must be certain not to overlook the fact that never in all human activity has there existed anything other than such cynicism, and that all idealistic, illusory webs are spun by this cynicism.

ii THE SUPERMAN

10.

ALL STRIVING of mankind, as of every living thing, exists for the satisfying, in the very best way, of impulses and instincts implanted by nature. When human beings strive toward morality, justice, knowledge and art, this is done because morality, justice, and so forth, are means by which these human instincts can develop themselves according to their nature. The instincts would atrophy without these means. Now it is a peculiarity of the human being that he *forgets* this connection between his life needs and his natural impulses, and regards these means for a natural, powerful life as something with unconditional *intrinsic* value. Man then says that morality, justice, knowledge, and so on, must be attained for their own sakes. They do not have an intrinsic value in that they serve life, but rather that life first receives value when it strives toward these ideal possessions. Man does not exist to live according to his instincts, like an animal, but that he may ennoble his instincts by placing them at the service of higher purposes. In this way man comes to the point where he worships as ideals what he had first created for the satisfaction of his impulses, ideals which first give his life true inspiration. He demands *subjugation* to ideals which he values more highly than himself. He frees himself from the mother ground of reality and wishes to give his existence a higher meaning and purpose. He invents an unnatural origin for his ideals. He calls them "God's will," the "eternal, moral laws." He wishes to strive after "truth for truth's sake," "virtue for virtue's sake." He considers himself a good human being only when he has supposedly succeeded in controlling his egotism, that is, his natural instincts, and in following one ideal goal selflessly. For such an idealist, *that* man is considered ignoble and "evil" who has not attained such self control.

Now all ideals originally stem from natural instincts. Also what Christ considers as virtue, which God has revealed to Him, man has originally discovered as satisfying some instinct or other. The natural origin is forgotten, and the divine imagined and superimposed. A similar situation exists in relation to those virtues which the philosophers and preachers of morality set up.

If mankind had only *sound* instincts and would determine their ideals according to them, then this theoretical error about the origin of these ideals would not be harmful. The idealists, of course, would have false opinions about the origin of their goals, but in themselves these goals would be sound, and life would have to flourish. But there are unsound instincts which are not directed toward strengthening and fostering life, but rather toward weakening and stunting it. These take control of the so-called theoretical confusion and make it into the practical life purpose. *They* mislead man into saying, A perfect man is not the one who wants to serve himself and his life, but the one who devotes himself to the realization of an ideal. Under the influence of these instincts, the human being does not merely remain at the point where he erroneously ascribes an unnatural or supernatural origin to his ideals, but he actually makes such ideals part of himself, or takes over from others those which do *not* serve the necessities of life. He no longer strives to bring to light the forces lying within his own personality, but he lives according to a pattern which has been forced upon him. Whether he takes this goal from a religion or whether he himself determines it on the basis of certain assumptions *not* lying within his own nature, is of no importance. The philosopher who has in mind a universal purpose for mankind, and from this purpose directs his moral ideals, lays just as many fetters upon human nature as the originator of a religion who says to mankind, This is the goal which God has set for you, and this you must follow. It is also of no importance whether man intends to become an image of God or whether he invents an ideal of the "perfect human being," and resembles this as much as possible. Only the *single* human being, and only the impulses and instincts of this single human being are real. Only when he directs his attention to the needs of his own person, can man experience what is good for his life. The single human being does not become "perfect" when he denies himself and resembles a model, but when he brings to reality that within him which strives toward realization. Human activity does not first acquire meaning because it serves an impersonal, external purpose; it has its meaning in itself.

The anti-idealist of course will also see in unsound human activity an instinctive expression of man's primeval instincts. He knows that only out of instinct can the human being accomplish even what is contrary to instinct. But he will of course attack that which is against instinct, just as the doctor attacks a sickness, although the doctor knows that the sickness has arisen out of certain natural causes. Therefore, we may not accuse the anti-idealist by saying, You assert that everything toward which man strives, therefore all ideals as well, have originated naturally; and yet you attack idealism. Indeed, ideals arise just as naturally as sickness, but the healthy human being fights idealism just as he fights sickness. The idealist, however, regards ideals as something which must be cherished and protected.

According to Nietzsche's opinion, the belief that man will become perfect only when he serves "higher" goals is something that must be *overcome*. Man must recollect and know that he has created ideals only to serve *himself*. To live according to nature is healthier than to chase after ideals which supposedly do not originate out of reality. The human being who does not serve impersonal goals, but who looks for the purpose and meaning of his existence in himself, who makes his own such virtues as serve the unfoldment of his own power, and the perfection of his own might—Nietzsche values this human being more highly than the selfless idealist.

This it is what he propounds through his *Zarathustra*. The sovereign *individuum* which knows that it can live only out of its own nature and which sees its personal goal in a life configuration which fits its own being: for Nietzsche this is the *superman*, in contrast to the human being who believes that life has been given to him as a gift to serve a purpose lying outside of himself.

Zarathustra teaches the *superman*, that is, the human being who understands how to live according to nature. He teaches those human beings who regard their virtues as their own creations; he tells them to despise those who value their virtues higher than themselves.

Zarathustra has gone into the loneliness to free himself from humility according to which men bow down before their virtues. He reappears among mankind only when he has learned to despise *those* virtues which fetter life and do not wish to serve life. He moves lightly like a dancer, for he follows only himself and his will, and disregards the lines which are indicated by the virtues. No longer does the belief rest heavily upon him that it is wrong to follow only himself. Now Zarathustra no longer sleeps in order to dream about ideals; he is a watcher who faces reality in freedom. For him the human being who has lost himself and lies in the dust before his own creations, is like a polluted stream. For him the superman is an ocean which takes this stream into itself without becoming impure. For the superman has found himself; he recognizes *himself* as the master and creator of his virtues. Zarathustra has experienced grandeur in that all those virtues which are placed *above* the human being have become repugnant to him.

"What is the greatest which you can experience? It is the hour of great contempt, the hour in which your happiness becomes repugnance, and likewise your intellect and your virtue."

11.

The wisdom of Zarathustra is not in accord with the thinking of the "modern cultured person." The latter would like to make all human beings equal. If all strive after only one goal, they say, then there is contentment and happiness upon earth. They require that man should restrain his special, personal wishes, and serve only the whole, the universal happiness. Peace and tranquillity will then reign upon earth. If everyone has the same needs, then no one disturbs the orbits of others. The individual should not regard himself and his individual goals, but everyone should live according to their once-determined pattern. All individual living should vanish, and all become part of a universal world order.

"No shepherd and *one* flock! Everyone desires the same, everyone is equal; he who feels otherwise goes voluntarily into the madhouse."

" 'Formerly all the world was insane,' say the best of them, and blink.

"People are clever and know all that has happened, so there is no end to their mocking. People still quarrel, but are soon reconciled; otherwise it disturbs the digestion."

Zarathustra had been a lone-dweller too long to pay homage to such wisdom. He had heard the peculiar tones which sound from within the personality when man stands apart from the noise of the market place where one person merely repeats the words of another. And he would like to shout into the ears of human beings, Listen to the voices which sound forth in each individual among you. For only those voices are in accord with nature which tell each one of what he alone is capable. An enemy of life, of the rich full life, is the one who allows these voices to resound unheard, and who listens to the common cry of mankind. Zarathustra will not speak to the friends of the equality of all mankind. They can only misunderstand him. For they would believe that his superman is that ideal model which all of them should resemble. But Zarathustra wishes to make no prescriptions of what men should be; he will refer each one only to himself, and will say to him, Depend upon yourself, follow only yourself, put yourself above virtue, wisdom, and knowledge. Zarathustra speaks to those who wish to find *themselves,* not to a multitude who search for a common goal; his words are intended for those companions who, like him, go their own way. They alone understand him because they know that he does not wish to say, Look, there is the superman, become like him, but, Behold, I have searched for *myself;* I am as I teach you to be; go likewise and search for your own self; then you have the superman.

"To the one who dwells alone will I sing my song and to the twain-dweller; and unto him who still has ears for the unheard, his heart will I burden with my happiness."

The Superman

12.

Two animals, the serpent, the wisest, and the eagle, the proudest, accompany Zarathustra. They are the symbols of his instincts. Zarathustra values wisdom because it teaches the human being to find the hidden paths to reality; it teaches him to know what he needs for life. And Zarathustra also loves pride because pride arouses self-estimation in the human being, through which he comes to regard himself as the meaning and purpose of his existence. Pride does not place his wisdom, his virtue, above his own self, in favor of "higher, more sacred" goals. Still, rather than lose pride Zarathustra would lose wisdom.

For wisdom which is not accompanied by pride does not regard itself as the work of man. The one who lacks pride and self-esteem, believes his wisdom has come to him as a gift from heaven. Such a one says, Man is a fool, and he has only as much wisdom as the heavens wish to grant him.

"And should my wisdom abandon me—Oh, it loves to fly away!—may my pride then still fly with my foolishness!"

13.

The human spirit must pass through three metamorphoses until he finds himself. This is Zarathustra's teaching. At first the spirit is reverent. He calls that virtue which weighs him down. He lowers himself in order to raise his virtue. He says, All wisdom comes from God, and I must follow God's paths. God imposes the most difficult upon me to test my power, whether it proves itself to be strong and patient in its endurance. Only the one who is patient is strong. I will obey, says the spirit at this level, and will carry out the commandments of the world-spirit, without asking the meaning of these commandments. The spirit feels the pressure which a higher power exerts upon it. The spirit does not take its *own* paths, but the paths of him he serves.

The time arrives when the spirit becomes aware that no God speaks to him. Then he wishes to be free, and to become master of his own world. He searches after a thread of direction for his destiny. He no longer asks the world spirit how he should arrange his own life. Rather, he strives after a firm command, after a sacred "you shall." He looks for a yardstick by which he can measure the worth of things. He searches for a sign of differentiation between good and evil. There must be a rule for my life which is not dependent on me, on my own will: so speaks the spirit at this level. To this rule will I submit myself. I am free, the spirit means to say, but only free to obey such a rule.

At this level, the spirit conquers. It becomes like the child at play, who does not ask, How *shall* I do this or that, but who merely carries out his own will, who follows only his own self. "The spirit now demands *his own* will; he who is lost in the world has now won *his own* world."

"I named for you three metamorphoses of the spirit: How the spirit became a camel, the camel a lion, and the lion at last, a child. Thus spake Zarathustra."

14.

What do the wise desire who place virtue above man?

asks Zarathustra. They say, Only he who has done his duty, he who has followed the sacred "thou shalt," can have peace of soul. Man shall be virtuous so that he may dream of fulfilled duty, about fulfilled ideals, and feel no pangs of conscience. The virtuous say that a man with pangs of conscience resembles one who is asleep and whose rest is disturbed by bad dreams.

"Few know it, but one must have all virtues to sleep well. Do I bear false witness, do I commit adultery?

"Do I lust after my neighbor's wife? All this is incompatible with good sleep.

"Peace with God and with thy neighbor: this is what good sleep needs. And peace also with thy neighbor's devil! Otherwise it will haunt you at night."

The virtuous person does not do what his impulse tells him, but what produces his peace of soul. He lives so that he may peacefully dream about life. It is even more pleasant for him when his sleep, which he calls peace of soul, is disturbed by no dreams. This means that it is most pleasant for the virtuous person when from some source or other he receives rules for his actions, and for the rest, he can enjoy his peace. "His wisdom is called, Wake, in order to sleep well. And indeed, if life had no meaning, and I should have to choose nonsense, to me this would be the most worthy nonsense to choose," says Zarathustra.

For Zarathustra also there was a time when he believed that a spirit dwelling outside of the world, a God, had created the world. Zarathustra imagined him to be an unsatisfied, suffering God. To create satisfaction for himself, to free himself from his suffering, God created the world;

Zarathustra thought this, once upon a time. But he learned to understand that this is an illusion which he himself had created. "O you brothers, this God whom I created, was the work of a man and illusion of man, like all gods!" Zarathustra has learned to use his senses and to observe the world. And he becomes satisfied with the world; no longer do his thoughts sweep into the world beyond. Formerly he was blind, and could not see the world. For this reason he looked for salvation outside of the world. But Zarathustra has learned *to see* and to recognize that the world has meaning in itself.

"My ego taught me a new pride, which I teach mankind: not to hide the head in the sand of celestial things, but to carry it freely, a terrestrial head, which carries meaning for the earth."

15.

The idealists have split man into body and soul, have divided all existence into idea and reality. And they have made the soul, the spirit, the idea, into something especially valuable in order that they may despise the reality, the body all the more. But Zarathustra says, There is but *one* reality, but one body, and the soul is only something in the body, the ideal is only something in reality. Body and soul of man are *a unity;* body and spirit spring from *one* root. The spirit is there only because a body is there, which has strength to develop the spirit in itself. As the plant unfolds the blossom from itself, so the body unfolds the spirit from itself.

"Behind your thinking and your feeling, my brother,

stands a mighty master, an unknown wise one: he is called self. He lives within your body, he is your body."

The one with a sense for reality searches for the spirit, for the soul, in and about the real. He looks for intellect in the real; only he who considers reality as lacking in spirituality, as merely "natural," as "coarse"—he gives the spirit, the soul a special existence. He makes reality merely the dwelling place of the spirit. But such a one also lacks the sense for the perception of the spirit itself. Only because he does not see the spirit in the reality does he search for it elsewhere.

"There is more intelligence in your body than in your best wisdom."

"The body is one great intelligence, a plurality with *one* meaning, a war and a peace, a herd and a shepherd.

"An instrument of your body is also your small intelligence, my brother, which you call spirit, a small instrument and a toy of your great intelligence."

He is a fool who would tear the blossom from the plant and believe the broken blossom will still develop into fruit. He is also a fool who would separate the spirit from nature and believe such a separated spirit can still create.

Human beings with sick instincts have undertaken the separation of spirit and body. A sick instinct can only say, My kingdom is not of this world. The kingdom of a sound instinct is *only this world*.

16.

But what ideals have they not created, these despisers of reality! If we look them in the eye, these ideals of the ascetics, who say, Turn your gaze away from this world, and look toward the other world, what then is the meaning of these ascetic ideals? With this question, and the suppositions with which he answers them, Nietzsche has let us look into the very depths of his heart, left unsatisfied by the more modern Western culture. (*Genealogie der Moral*, Section 3)

When an *artist* like Richard Wagner, for example, becomes a follower of the ascetic ideal during his last period of creativity, this does not have too much significance. The artist places his entire life *above* his creations. He looks down from above upon his realities. He creates realities which are not his reality. "A Homer would not have created an Achilles, nor Goethe a Faust, if Homer had been an Achilles, or if Goethe had been a Faust." (*Genealogy*, 3rd Section, ¶ 4). Now when such an artist once begins to take his own existence seriously, wishes to change himself and his personal opinion into reality, it is no wonder when something very unreal arises. Richard Wagner completely reversed his knowledge about his art when he became familiar with Schopenhauer's philosophy. Previously, he considered music as a means of expression which required something to which it gives expression—the drama. In his *Opera and Drama*, written in 1851, he says that the greatest error into which one can fall with regard to the opera is,

"That a means of expression (the music) is made the purpose, but the purpose of expression (the drama) is made the means."

He professed another opinion after he had come to

know Schopenhauer's teaching about music. Schopenhauer is of the opinion that through music, the essence of the thing itself speaks to us. The eternal *Will*, which lives in all things, becomes embodied in all other arts only through images, through the ideas; music is no mere picture of the will: the will reveals itself in it *directly*. What appears to us in all our reflections only as image, the eternal ground of all existence, the will, Schopenhauer believed he heard directly in the sound of music. A message from the other world is brought to Schopenhauer by music. This point of view affected Richard Wagner. Thus he lets music no longer be a means of expression of real human passions as they are embodied in drama, but as a "sort of mouthpiece for the *intrinsic essence* of things, a telephone from the other world." Richard Wagner now no longer believed in expressing reality in tones; "henceforth he talked not only music, this ventriloquist of God, but he talked metaphysics: no wonder that one day he talked *ascetic ideals*." (*Genealogy*, 3rd Section, ¶ 5).

If Richard Wagner had merely changed his opinion about the significance of music, then Nietzsche would have had no reason to reproach him. At most Nietzsche could then say, Besides his art works Wagner has also created all sorts of wrong theories about art. But that during the last period of his creativity Wagner embodied in his art works the Schopenhauer belief in the world beyond, that he utilized his music to glorify the flight from reality, this was distasteful to Nietzsche.

The Case of Wagner means nothing when it is a question of the significance of the glorification of the world beyond at the expense of this world, when it is a question of the significance of ascetic ideals. Artists do not stand on their own feet. As Richard Wagner is dependent upon Schopenhauer, so "at all times were the artists valets to a morality, a philosophy or a religion."

It is quite different when the philosophers represent a contempt of reality, of ascetic ideals. They do this out of a deep instinct.

Schopenhauer betrayed this instinct through the description which he gives of the creating and enjoying of a work of art. "That the *work of art* makes the understanding of ideas, in which the aesthetic enjoyment consists, so much easier, depends not merely upon the fact that through emphasis of the material and discarding of the immaterial, art represents the things more clearly and more characteristically, but it depends much more upon the fact that the complete silence of the will, necessary for *the objective understanding of the nature of things, is achieved with most certainty through the fact that the object looked upon does not lie at all within the realm of things which are capable of a relationship to will."* (Additions to the third book of *Welt als Wille und Vorstellung,* The World as Will and Reflection, Chapter 30) "When an outer circumstance or an inner soul mood lifts us suddenly out of the endless stream of willing, then knowledge takes away the slavish service of the will when attention is no longer directed to the motive of willing, but comprehends the things free from their relationship to will, that is, *without interest, without subjectivity,* considers them purely objectively, completely surrendered to them insofar as

The Superman

they are mere representations, not insofar as they are motives; then is begun the painless state which Epicurus praised as the highest good and as the state of the gods. Then, during that moment, we are freed from the contemptible pressure of the will; we celebrate the sabbath of the will's hard labor, the wheel of Ixion stands still." *Ibid.* ¶ 38)

This is a description of a type of aesthetic enjoyment which appears only with philosophers. Nietzsche contrasts this with another description "which a real spectator and artist has made—Stendahl," who calls the beautiful *une promesse de bonheur*. Schopenhauer would like to exclude all will interest, all real life, when it is a question of the observation of a work of art, and would enjoy it only with the *spirit;* Stendhal sees in the work of art *a promise of happiness,* therefore, an indication for life, and sees the value of art in this connection of art with life.

Kant demanded that a beautiful work of art should please *without interest:* that is, that the work of art lift us out of the reality of life and give us purely spiritual enjoyment.

What does the philosopher look for in artistic enjoyment? *Escape* from reality. The philosopher wants to be transferred into an atmosphere foreign to reality, through works of art. Thereby he betrays his basic instinct. The philosopher feels most satisfied during those moments when he can be freed from reality. His attitude toward aesthetic enjoyment proves that he does not love this reality.

In their theories the philosophers do not tell us what

the spectator whose interests are turned toward life, demands of a work of art, but only what is of interest to themselves. And for the philosopher the turning away from life is very useful. He does not wish to have his hidden thought paths crossed by reality. Thinking flourishes better when the philosopher turns away from life. Then it is no wonder when this philosophical basic instinct becomes a mood almost hostile to life. We find that such a soul mood is cultivated by the majority of philosophers. And a very close connection exists between the fact that the philosopher develops and elaborates his own antipathy toward life into a teaching, and the fact that all men acknowledge such a teaching. Schopenhauer did this. He found that the noise of the world disturbed his thought work. He felt that one could *meditate* about reality better when one escaped from this reality. At the same time, he forgot that all thinking about reality has value only when it springs from this reality. He did not observe that the withdrawing of the philosopher from reality can occur only when the philosophical thoughts which have arisen out of this separation from life can be of higher service to life. When the philosopher wishes to force the basic instinct, which is only of value to him as a philosopher, upon the whole of mankind, then he becomes an enemy to life.

The philosopher who does not regard the flight from the world as a means of creating thoughts friendly to the world, but as a purpose, as a goal in itself, can only create worthless things. The true philosopher flees from reality on the one hand, only that he may penetrate deeper into it on the other. But it is conceivable that this basic instinct can easily mislead the philosopher into considering the flight from the world as such to be valuable. Then the philosopher becomes a representative of world negation. He teaches a turning away from life, the ascetic ideal. He finds that "A certain asceticism, a hard and joyous renunciation of the best will, belongs to the favorable conditions of highest spirituality, as well as to their most natural consequences. So from the beginning it is not surprising if the ascetic ideal is never treated, particularly by the philosophers, without some objections." (*Genealogy*, Part III, ¶ 9)

17.

The ascetic ideals of the *priests* have another origin. What develops in the philosopher as the luxuriant growth of an impulse he considers justified, forms the basic ideal of the working and creating of the priest. The priest sees error in the surrender of the human being to real life; he demands that one respect *this* life less in face of another life, which is directed by higher than merely natural forces. The priest denies that real life has meaning in itself, and he challenges the idea that this meaning is given to it through an inocculation of a higher will. He sees life in the temporal as imperfect, and he places opposite to it an eternal, perfect life. The priest teaches a turning away from the temporal and entering into the eternal, the unchangeable. As especially significant of the way of thinking of the priest, I would like to quote a few sentences from the famous book, *Die Deutsche Theologie,* German Theology, which stems from the fourteenth century, and about which Luther says that from no other book, with the exception of the Bible, and the writings of St. Augustine, has he learned more about what God, Christ, and man are, than from this. Schopenhauer also finds that the spirit of Christianity is expressed more perfectly and more powerfully in this book than elsewhere. After the writer, who is unknown to us, has explained that all things of the world are imperfect and incomplete, in contrast to the perfect, "which in itself and in its essence comprehended all things and decided all things, and without which, and outside of which no true being exists, and in which all things have their being," he continues that man can penetrate into this being only if he has lost all "creaturedom, creationdom, egodom, selfdom, and everything similar," nullifying them in himself. What has flowed out of the perfect, and what the human being recognizes as his real world, is described in the following way: "That is no true being, and has no being other than in the perfect, but it is an accident or a radiance, and an illusion which is no being, or has no being other than in the fire from which the radiance streams, or in the sun, or in the light. The book says, as do belief, and truth, sin is nothing but that the creature turns away from the unchangeable good and turns toward the changeable, that is, that it turns away from the perfect to the incomplete and imperfect, and most of all to itself. Now note, If this creature takes on something good as existence, life, knowledge, understanding, possession, in short, all those things which one calls good, and thinks that *they are good, or that it itself is good or that good belongs* to it, or stems from it, just as often as this happens, so often does it turn itself away. In what way did the devil do anything different—or what was his fall and turning away—than that *he thought he was something, and that that something was his, and also that something belonged to him?* This acceptance, and his 'I' and his 'me,' his 'to me,' and his 'mine'—all this was his turning away and his fall. Thus it is still . . . For all that one considers good or would call good, belongs to no one, except to the eternal, true Good, who is God alone, and he who takes possession of it does wrong, and is against God." (Chapters 1, 2, 4, of *German Theology*, 3rd edition)

These sentences express the attitude of *every* priest. They express the particular character of the priesthood. And this character is exactly the opposite of that which Nietzsche describes as the more valuable, more worthy of life. The more highly valued type of man wants to be everything that he is, through himself alone; he wants all that he considers good and calls good to belong to no one but himself.

But this mediocre attitude is no exception. It is one of "the most widespread, oldest facts that exist." Read from a distant star, perhaps, the writing of our earth existence would lead to the conclusion that the earth is the really *ascetic star*, a corner of dissatisfied, proud, disagreeable creatures who cannot free themselves from a deep dissatisfaction with themselves, with the earth, and with all life." (*Genealogy*, Part III, ¶ 11) For this reason, the ascetic priest is a necessity, since the majority of human beings suffer from an "obstruction and fatigue" of life-forces because they suffer from reality. The ascetic priest is the comforter and physician of those who suffer from life. He comforts them by saying to them, This life from which you are suffering is not the real life; for those who suffer from this life, the true life is much more easily attainable than for the healthy, who depend upon this life and surrender themselves to it. Through such expressions the priest breeds contempt for, and betrayal of the real life. He finally brings forth the state of mind which says that to obtain the true life, the real life must be *denied*. In the spreading of this mood, the ascetic priest seeks his strength. Through the training of this soul mood, he eliminates a great danger which threatens the healthy, the strong, the ego-conscious, from the unhappy, the suppressed, the broken-down. The latter hate the healthy and the happy in body and soul, who take their strength from nature. This hatred, which must express itself, is that the weak wage a continuous war of annihilation against the strong. This the priest tries to suppress. Therefore, he represents the strong as those who lead a life which is worthless and unworthy of human beings, and, on the other hand, asserts that true life is obtainable only by those who were hurt by the earth life. "The ascetic priest must be accepted by us as the predestined saviour, shepherd, and champion of the sick herd; in this way we understand his tremendous historic mission for the first time. *The domination over the sufferers* is his kingdom. His instinct directs him toward it. In this he finds his own special art, his mastery, his form of happiness." (*Genealogy*, Part III, ¶15).

The Superman

It is no wonder that such a way of thinking finally leads to the fact that its followers not only despise life, but work directly toward its destruction. If it is said to man that only the sufferer, the weak, can really attain a higher life, then in the end the suffering, the weakness will be *sought*. To bring pain to oneself, to kill the will within oneself completely, will become the goal of life. The victims of this soul-mood are the saints. "Complete chastity and denial of all pleasure are for him who strives toward real holiness; throwing away of all possessions, desertion of every dwelling, of all dependents, deep, complete loneliness, spent in profound, silent reflection, with voluntary penitence and frightful, slow self-torture, to the complete mortification of the will, which finally dies voluntarily by hunger, or by walking toward crocodiles, by throwing oneself from sacred mountain heights in the Himalayas, by being buried alive, or by throwing oneself under the wheels of the Juggernaut driven among the statues of the idols, accompanied by the song, jubilation and dance of the Bajadere," these are the ultimate fruits of the ascetic state of mind. (Schopenhauer, *Welt als Wille und Vorstellung,* World as Will and Representation, ¶68).

This way of thinking has arisen out of the suffering of life, and it directs its weapons against life. When the healthy person, filled with joy of life, is infected by it, then it destroys the sound, strong instincts within him. Nietzsche's work towers above this in that in face of this teaching he brings out the value of another point of view for the healthy, for those of well-being. May the malformed, the ruined, find their salvation in the teaching of the ascetic priests; Nietzsche will gather the healthy about him, and will give them advice which will please them more than all ideals which are inimical to life.

18.

The ascetic ideal is implanted in the guardians of modern science also. Of course, this science boasts that it has thrown all old beliefs overboard, and that it holds fast only to reality. It will consider nothing valid which cannot be counted, calculated, weighed, seen or grasped. That through this "one degrades existence to a slavish exercise in arithmetic and a game for mathematicians," is of indifference to the modern scholar. (*Fröhliche Wissenschaft,* Joyful Science, ¶ 373). Such a scholar does not ascribe to himself the right to interpret the happenings of the world, which pass before his senses and his intellect, so that he can control them with his thinking. He says, Truth must be independent of my art of interpretation, and it is not up to me to create truth; instead, I must allow the world to dictate truth to me through world phenomena.

The point to which this modern science finally comes when it contains within itself all arranging of world phenomena, has been expressed by Richard Wahle, a follower of this science, in a book which has just appeared: *Das Ganze der Philosophie und ihr Ende,* The Totality of Philosophy and its End. "What can the spirit who peers into this world-house and turns over the questions about the nature and goal of happenings, find as an answer

The Superman

at last? It has happened that as he stood so apparently in opposition to the world surrounding him, he became disentangled, and in a flight from all events, merged with all events. He no longer 'knew' the world. He said, I am not sure that those who know exist; perhaps there are simply events. They occur, of course, in such a way that the concept of a knowing could develop prematurely and without justification, and 'concepts' have sprouted up to bring light into these events, but they are will-o-the-wisps, souls of the desires for knowing, pitiful postulates of an empty form of knowledge, saying nothing in their evidence. *Unknown factors must hold sway in the transitions.* Darkness was spread over their nature. Events are the veil of the nature of truth."

That the human personality, out of its own capacities, can instill meaning into the happenings of reality, and can supplement the *unknown factors* which rule in the transitions of events: modern scholars do not think at all about this. They do not want to interpret the flight from appearances by ideals which stem from their own personality. They want merely to observe and describe the appearances, but not interpret them. They want to remain with the factual, and will not allow the creative fantasy to make a dismembered picture of reality.

When an imaginative natural scientist, for example, Ernst Haeckel, out of the results of individual observations, formulates a total picture of the evolution of organic life on earth, then these fanatics of factuality throw themselves upon him, and accuse him of transgression against truth. The pictures which he sketched about life in nature, they cannot see with their eyes or touch with their hands. They prefer the impersonal judgment to that which is colored by the spirit of the personality. They would prefer to exclude the personality completely from their observations.

It is the ascetic ideal which controls the fanatics of factuality. They would like a truth *beyond* the personal individual judgment. What the human being can "imagine into" things, does not concern these fanatics. "Truth" to them is something absolutely perfect—a God; man should discover it, should surrender to it, but should not create it. At present, the natural scientists and the historians are enthused by the same spirit of ascetic ideals. Everywhere they enumerate in order to describe facts, and nothing more. All arranging of facts is forbidden. All personal judgment is to be suppressed.

Atheists are also found among these modern scholars. But these atheists are freer spirits than their contemporaries who believe in God. The existence of God cannot be proven by means of modern science. Indeed, one of the brilliant minds of modern science, Du Bois-Reymond, expressed himself thus about the acceptance of a "world-soul:" before the natural scientist decides upon such an acceptance he demands "That somewhere in the world, there be shown to him, bedded in nerve ganglia and nourished with warm, arterial blood under the correct pressure, a bundle of cell ganglia and nerve fibers, depending in size on the spiritual capacity of the soul." (*Grenzen des Naturerkennens*, Limits of Natural Science, page 44). Modern science rejects the belief in God because this belief cannot exist beside their belief in "objective truth." This "objective truth," however, is nothing but a new God who has been victorious over the old one. "Unqualified, honest atheism (and we breathe only its air; we, the most intellectual human being of this age) does *not* stand in opposition to that (ascetic) ideal to the extent that it appears to; rather, it is one of its final phases of evolution, one of its ultimate forms, one of its logical consequences. It is the awe-inspiring *catastrophe* of a two thousand year training in truth, which finally forbids itself *the lie of the belief in God.*" (*Genealogy*, Part III, ¶27). Christ seeks truth in God because He considers God the source of all truth. The modern atheist rejects the belief in God because his god, his ideal of truth, forbids him this belief. In God the modern spirit sees a human creation; in "truth" he sees something which has come into being by itself without any human interference. The really "free spirit" goes still further. He asks, *"What is the meaning of all will for truth?"* Why truth? For all truth arises in that man ponders over the appearance of the world, and formulates thoughts about things. Man himself is the creator of truth. The "free spirit" arrives at the awareness of his own creation of truth. He no longer regards truth as something to which he subordinates himself; he looks upon it as his own creation.

19.

People endowed with weak, malformed instincts of perception do not dare to attach meaning to world appearances out of the concept-forming power of their personality. They wish the "laws of nature" to stand before their senses as actual facts. A subjective world-picture, formed by the instrumentality of the human mind, appears worthless to them. But the mere observation of world events presents us with only a disconnected, not a detailed world picture. To the mere observer of things, no object, no event, appears more important, more significant than another. When we have considered it, the rudimentary organ of an organism which perhaps appears to have no significance for the evolution of life, stands there with exactly the same demand upon our attention as does the most noble part of the organism, so long as we look merely at the actual facts. Cause and effect are appearances following upon each other, which merge into each other without being separated by anything, so long as we *merely observe* them. Only when with our thinking, we begin to separate the appearances which have merged into each other, and relate them to each other intellectually, does *a regular connection* become visible. Thinking alone explains one appearance as cause and another as effect. We see a raindrop fall upon the earth and produce a groove. A being which is unable to think will not see cause and effect here, but only a sequence of appearances. A thinking being isolates the appearances, relates the isolated facts, and labels the one factor as cause, the other as effect. Through observation the intellect is stimulated to produce thoughts and to fuse these thoughts with the observed facts into a meaningful world-picture. Man does this because he wishes to control the sum of his observations with his thoughts. A thought-vacuum before him,

The Superman

presses upon him like an unknown power. He opposes this power and conquers it by making it conceivable. All counting, weighing and calculating of appearances also comes about for the same reason. It is the *will to power* which lives itself out in this impulse for knowledge. (I have represented a process of knowledge in detail in my two writings. *Wahrheit und Wissenschaft,* Truth and Knowledge and *Die Philosophie der Freiheit,* The Philosophy of Spiritual Activity.)

The dull, weak intellect does not want to admit to himself that it is he himself who interprets the appearances as expression of his striving toward power. He considers his interpretation also as an actual fact. And he asks, How does a man come to find such an actual fact in reality? He asks, for example, How is it that the intellect can recognize cause and effect in two appearances, one following upon the other? All theorists of knowledge, from Locke, Hume, Kant, down to the present time, have occupied themselves with this question. The subtleties which they have applied to this examination, have remained unfruitful. The explanation is given in the striving of the human intellect toward power. The question is not at all, Are judgments, thoughts about appearances, possible? but, Does the human intellect need such judgments? He needs them, hence he uses them, not because they are possible. It depends upon this: "To understand that for the sake of the preservation of creatures like ourselves such judgments must be *believed* to be true, though naturally they still may be *false* judgments!" (*Jenseits von Gut und Böse,* Beyond Good and Evil, ¶11) "And fundamentally we are inclined to assert that the most erroneous judgments are the most indispensible for us; that man could not live without belief in logical fiction, without measuring reality by the purely invented world of the unconditional, likening one's self to one's self, without a constant falsification of the world through number; that renunciation of false judgments would be a renunciation of life, a negation of life." (*Ibid.*, ¶ 4). Whoever regards this saying as a paradox, should remind himself how fruitful is the use of geometry in relation to reality, although nowhere in the world are really geometric, regular lines, planes, etc., to be found.

When the dull, weak intellect understands that all judgments about things stem from within him, are all produced by him, and are fused with the observations, then he does not have the courage to use these judgments unreservedly. He says, Judgments of this kind cannot transmit knowledge of the "true essence" of things to us. Therefore, this "true essence" remains excluded from our knowledge.

The weak intellect tries in still another way to prove that no security can be attained through human knowledge. He says, The human being sees, hears, touches things and events. Thereby he perceives impressions of his sense organs. When he perceives a color, a sound, then he can only say, My eye, my ear are determined in a certain way to perceive color and tone. Man perceives nothing *outside of himself* except a determination, a modification of his own organs. In perceiving, his eyes, his ears, etc., become stimulated to feel in a certain way; they are placed in a certain condition. The human being perceives this condition of his own organs as colors, tones, odors, etc. In all perceiving, the human being perceives only his own conditions. What he calls the outer world is composed only of his own conditions; therefore, in a real sense it is *his work*. He does not know the things which cause him to spin the outer world out of himself; he only knows the effects upon his organs. In this light, the world appears like a dream which is dreamed by the human being, and is occasioned by something unknown.

When this thought is brought to its consequential conclusion, it brings with it the following afterthought. Man knows only his own organs, insofar as he perceives them; they are parts of his world of perception. And man becomes conscious of his own self only to the extent that he spins pictures of the world out of himself. He perceives dream pictures, and in the midst of these dream pictures, an "I," by which these dream pictures pass; every dream picture appears to be an accompaniment of this "I." One can also say that each dream picture appears in the midst of the dream world, always in relation to this "I." This "I" clings to these dream pictures as determination, as characteristic. Consequently, as a determination of dream pictures, it is a dream-like being itself. J. G. Fichte sums up this point of view in these words: "What develops through this knowing, and out of this knowing, is but a knowing. But all knowing is merely reflection, and something is always demanded of it which conforms to the picture. This demand cannot be satisfied by knowledge; and a system of knowledge is necessarily a system of mere pictures, *without any reality, without significance, and without purpose."* For Fichte, "all reality" is a wonderful "dream without a life, which is being dreamed about, without a spirit who dreams." It is a dream "which is connected with itself in a dream." *(Bestimmung des Menschen,* Mission of Man, 2nd Book)

What meaning has this whole chain of thoughts? A weak intellect, which does not dare to give meaning to the world out of himself, looks for this meaning in the world of observations. Of course, he cannot find it there because mere observation is void of thoughts.

A strong, productive intellect uses his world of concepts to interpret the observations. The weak, unproductive intellect declares himself to be too powerless to do this, and says, I can find no sense in the appearances of the world; they are mere pictures which pass by me. The meaning of existence, therefore, must be looked for outside, beyond the world of appearances. Because of this, the world of appearances, that is, the human reality, is explained as a dream, an illusion, a *Nothing,* and "the true being" of appearances is searched for in a "thing in itself," for which no observation, no knowledge is sufficient, that is, about which the knower can form no idea. Therefore, for the knower, this "true being" is a completely empty thought, the thought about *a Nothing.* For those philosophers who speak about the "thing in itself," a dream is a world of appearances. But this *Nothing* they regard as the "true being" of the world of appearances. The whole philosophical movement which speaks about the "thing in itself," and which, in more modern times, leans mainly upon Kant, is the belief in this *Nothing;* it is *philosophical nihilism.*

20.

When the strong spirit looks for the cause of a human action and achievement, he will always find it in the will power of the individual personality. But the human being with a weak, timid intellect will not admit this. He doesn't feel himself sufficiently strong to make himself master and guide of his own actions. He interprets the impulses which guide him as the commandments of another power. He does not say, I act as I want to act, but he says, I act according to a law which I *must obey.* He does not wish to *command himself;* he wishes *to obey.* At one level of their development, human beings see their impulses to action as commandments of God; at another level, they believe that they are aware of a voice inside them, which commands them. In the latter case they do not dare to say, It is I myself who command; they assert, In me a higher will expresses itself. One person is of the opinion that it is his *conscience* which speaks to him in each individual case, and tells him how he should act, while another asserts that a categorical imperative commands him. Let us hear what J. G. Fichte says: "Something simply will happen because something just *must* happen; conscience now demands of me that it happen, and simply for this reason I am here; I am to realize it, and for that I have intellect. I am to achieve it, and for that I have strength." (*Ibid.,* Third Book) I mention J. G. Fichte's sayings with great pleasure because he maintained with iron consequence his opinion of the "weak and malformed." He maintained it to the very end. One can only realize where this opinion finally leads when one looks for it where it was thought through to the end; one cannot depend upon those who are incomplete thinkers, who think each thought only to the middle.

The fount of knowledge is not sought in individual personalities by those who think in the above mentioned way, but beyond personality in a "will in itself." Just this "will in itself" shall speak to the individual as "God's voice," as the "voice of conscience," as categorical imperative, and so on. This is to be the universal leader of human actions, and *the fount of all morality,* and is also to determine *the purpose of moral actions.* "I say that it is the commandment to action itself which gives me a purpose through itself. It is the same in me which urges me to think that I should act in such a way, urges me to believe that out of these actions something will result; it opens the view to another world." "As I live in *obedience,* at the same time I live in the reflection of its purposes; *I live in the better world which it promises me."* (*Ibid.,* Third Book) He who thinks thus, will not set a goal for himself; he will allow himself to be led to a goal by the higher will which he obeys. He will free himself from his own will, and will make himself into an instrument for "higher" purposes in words which express the highest achievements of obedience and humility known to him. Fichte described the abandonment to this "eternal will in itself." "Lofty, living Will, which no name names and no concept encompasses, may I raise my soul to you, for you and I are not separated. Your voice sounds within me; mine resounds in you; and *all my thoughts, when they are true and good, are thought within you.* In you, the incomprehensible, I become comprehensible to myself, and the world becomes perfectly comprehensible to me. All problems of my existence are solved, and the most complete harmony arises within my spirit"... "I veil my countenance before you. I lay my hand upon my mouth. As you yourself are, and as you appear to yourself, I can never understand, as certainly as I never could become you. After I have lived a thousand thousand spirit lives, I shall comprehend you as little as I do now in this hut upon earth." (*Ibid.,* Third Book)

Where this will is finally to lead man, the individual cannot know. Therefore the one who believes in this will confesses that he knows *nothing* about the final purposes of his actions. For such a believer in a higher will, the goals which the individual sets for himself, are not "true goals." Therefore, in place of the positive individual goals created by the *individuum,* he places a final purpose for the whole of mankind, the thought content of which, however, is a *Nothing.* Such a believer is *a moral nihilist.* He is caught in the worst kind of ignorance imaginable. Nietzsche wanted to deal with this type of ignorance in a special section of his incompleted work, *Der Wille zur Macht,* The Will to Power.

We find the praise of moral nihilism again in Fichte's *Bestimmung des Menschen,* Destiny of Man (Third Book): "I shall not attempt what is denied me by the very Being of Limitations, and I shall not attempt what would avail me nothing. What you yourself are, I do not care to know. But your relationships and your connections with me, the Specific, and toward everything Specific, lie open before my eyes; may I become what I must become! and all this surrounds me in more brilliant clarity than the consciousness of my own existence. *You create* within me the knowledge of my duty, of my destiny, in the order of intelligent beings; how, I know not, nor do I need to know. *You know, and you recognize* what I think and what I will; how you can know it, through what act you achieve this consciousness, *I understand nothing.* Yes, I know very well that the concept of an act and of a special act of consciousness is valid only for me, but not for you, Infinite Being. You govern because *you will* that my free obedience has consequences to all eternity; *the act of your willing I do not understand,* and only know that it is not similar to mine. *Your act* and your will itself is *a deed.* But the way you work is exactly opposite to that way which I alone am able to understand. *You live and you are* because you know, will, and effectuate, ever present in the limited intellect, *but you are not as I conceive a being to be through eternities."*

Nietzsche places opposite to moral nihilism those goals which the *creating* individual will places before itself. Zarathustra calls to the teachers of the gospel of submission:

"These teachers of the gospel of submission. Everywhere where there is smallness and sickness and dirt, there they creep like lice, and only my disgust prevents me from crushing them under foot.

The Superman

"Attend! This is my gospel for their ears: I am Zarathustra, the godless, who asks, Who is more godless than I, that I may rejoice in his teaching?

"I am Zarathustra, the godless; where do I find my equal? All those are my equals *who determine their will out of themselves, and who push all submission away from themselves.*"

21.

The strong personality which creates goals is disdainful of the execution of them. The weak personality, on the other hand, carries out only what the Divine Will, the "voice of conscience" or the "categorical imperative" says *Yes* to. That which is in accordance with this *Yes,* the weak person describes as *good,* that which is contrary to this *Yes,* it describes as *evil.* The strong personality cannot acknowledge this "good and evil," for he does not acknowledge that power from which the weak person allows his "good and evil" to be determined. What the strong person wills is for him *good;* he carries it through in spite of all opposing powers. What disturbs him in this execution, he tries to overcome. He does not believe that an "Eternal Will" guides the decisions of all individual wills toward a great harmony, but he believes that all human development comes out of the will-impasses of the individual personalities, and that an eternal war is waged between the expressions of individual wills, in which the stronger will always conquers the weaker.

The strong personality who lays down his own laws and sets his own goals, is described by the weaker and less courageous as evil, as sinful. He arouses fear, for he breaks through traditional ways; he calls that worthless which the weak person is accustomed to call valuable, and he invents the new, the previously unknown, which he describes as valuable. "Each individual action, each individual way of thinking causes shuddering; it is almost impossible to estimate exactly what those more uncommon, more select, more criminal spirits must have suffered in the course of history so that they were always regarded as bad, as dangerous, yes, even so that *they themselves considered themselves in this light*. Under the domination of custom, all originality of every kind has evoked a bad conscience. Up to this very time the heaven of the most admirable has become more darkened than it would have had to be." (*Morgenröte*, Dawn, p. 9)

The truly *free* spirit makes *original* decisions immediately; the unfree spirit decides in accordance with his background. "Morality is nothing more (specifically, *nothing more!*) than obedience to customs of whatever nature these may be; but customs are the *traditional* way of acting and evaluating." (*Ibid.*, p. 9). It is this tradition which is interpreted by the moralists as "eternal will," as "categorical imperative." But every tradition is the result of natural impulses, of lives of individuals, of entire tribes, nations, and so on. It is also the product of natural causes, for example, the condition of the weather in specific localities. The free spirit explains that he does not feel himself bound by such tradition. He has his individual drives and impulses, and feels that these are not less justified than those of others. He transforms these

The Superman

impulses into action as a cloud sends rain to the earth's surface when causes for this exist. The free spirit takes his stand *opposite to what tradition considers to be good and evil.* He *creates* his own good and evil for himself.

"When I came to men, I found them sitting there on an old presumption: they all assumed that they had long known what was *good* and *evil* for man.

"All debating about virtue seemed to them an old, worn-out affair, and he who wanted to sleep well, still spoke about good and evil before going to sleep.

"This sleepiness I disturbed by my teaching; what is good and what is evil, *nobody knows;* then let it be the creator.

"But that is he who *creates* man's goal and who gives meaning to the earth and to the future. It is he who first *brings it about* that there is something good and evil." (*Zarathustra,* 3rd Part, From the Old and New Tablets)

Besides this, when the free spirit acts according to tradition, he does this because he adopts the traditional motives, and because he does not consider it necessary in certain cases to put something new in place of the traditional.

22.

The strong person seeks his life's task in working out his creative *self.* This *self-seeking* differentiates him from the weak person who, in the *selfless* surrender to that which he calls "good," sees morality. The weak preach selflessness as the highest virtue, but their selflessness is only the consequence of their lack of creative power. If they had any creative self they would then have wished to manifest it. The strong person loves war because he needs war to manifest his creation in opposition to those powers hostile to him.

"Your enemy you shall seek, your war you shall wage, and as for your thoughts, if they succumb, then shall your very uprightness nevertheless attain triumph over their collapse!

"You shall love peace as a means to a new war, and a short peace more than a long one.

"I do not challenge you to work, but to fight. I do not challenge you to peace, but to victory. Your work be your struggle! Your peace be a victory!

"You say that the *good* circumstance may even sanctify war, but I say to you, it is the 'good' war which sanctifies every circumstance.

"War and courage have accomplished more great things than love for one's neighbor. Until now, not your sympathy but your courage has saved the unfortunate." (*Zarathustra*, 1st Part, About War and People of War)

The creative person acts without mercy and without regard for those who oppose. He has no cognizance of the virtue of those who suffer, namely, of sympathy. Out of his own power come his impulses to creativity, not out of his feelings for another's suffering. That power may conquer, for this he fights, not that suffering and weakness may be cared for. Schopenhauer has described the

The Superman

whole world as a hospital, and asked that the actions springing out of sympathy for suffering be considered as the highest virtue. Thereby he has expressed the morality of Christendom in another form than the latter itself has done. He who creates, though, does not feel himself destined to render these nursing services. The efficient ones, the healthy, cannot exist for the sake of the weak, the sick. Sympathy weakens power, courage, and bravery.

Sympathy seeks to maintain just what the strong wishes to overcome, that is, the weakness, the suffering. The victory of the strong over the weak is the meaning of all human as well as of all natural development. "Life in its *essence* is a usurping, a wounding, an overcoming of the strange, of all that is misfit and weak. Life is the suppressing, the hardening and forcing through of one's own forms, the embodying, and, in the least and mildest, the erupting in boils." (*Jenseits von Gut und Böse,* Beyond Good and Evil, ¶ 259).

"And do you not wish to be a dealer of destiny and unmerciful? How else can you be mine or conquer with me?"

"And if your hardness will not strike as lightning and cleave and cut, how then can you ever create with me?

"For the creators are hard, and it must seem to you a blessing to press your hand upon the millennia as if upon wax.

"A blessing to inscribe upon the will of millennia as if upon bronze, harder than bronze, more precious than bronze. Entirely hard is the most precious alone.

"This new tablet, O my brothers, I raise above you, thou shalt become *hard*." (*Zarathustra*, 3rd Part, From the Old and New Tablets)

The free spirit makes no demands upon sympathy. He would have to ask the one who would pity him, Do you consider me as weak, that I cannot bear my suffering by myself? For him, each expression of sympathy is humiliating. Nietzsche shows this aversion of the strong person toward sympathy in the fourth part of *Zarathustra*. In his wanderings Zarathustra arrives in a valley which is called "Snake Death." No living beings are found here. Only a kind of ugly green snake comes here in order to die. The "most ugly human being" has found this valley. He does not wish to be seen by anyone because of his ugliness. In this valley he sees no one besides God, but even His countenance he cannot bear. The consciousness that God's gaze has penetrated into all these regions becomes a burden for him. For this reason he has killed God, that is, he has killed the belief in God within himself. He has become an atheist because of his ugliness. When Zarathustra sees this human being, he is overcome by what he believed he had destroyed within himself forever: that is, sympathy for the most frightful ugliness. This becomes a temptation for Zarathustra, but very soon he rejects the feeling of sympathy and again becomes *hard*. The most ugly man says to him, "Your hardness honors my ugliness. I am too *rich* in ugliness to be able to bear the sympathy of any human being. Sympathy humiliates."

He who requires sympathy cannot stand alone, and the free spirit wishes to stand completely on his own.

23.

The weak are not content with pointing to the natural will to power as the cause of human actions. They do not merely seek for natural connections in human development, but they seek for the relationship of human action to what they call the "will in itself," the eternal, moral world order. They *accuse* the one who acts contrary to this world order. And they also are not satisfied to evaluate an action according to its natural consequences, but they claim that a guilty action also draws with it moral consequences, i.e., *punishment*. They consider themselves guilty if their actions are not in accord with the moral world order; they turn away in horror from the fount of evil in themselves, and they call this feeling *bad conscience*. The strong personality, on the other hand, does not consider all these concepts valid. He is concerned only with the natural consequences of actions. He asks, Of what value for life is my way of acting? Is it in accord with what I have willed? The strong cannot grieve when an action goes wrong, when the result does not accord with his intentions. But he does not blame himself. For he does not measure his way of acting by supernatural yardsticks. He knows that he has acted thus in accord with his natural impulses, and at most he can regret that these are not better. It is the same with his judgment regarding the actions of others. A *moral* evaluation of actions he does not grant. He is an amoralist.

What tradition considers to be *evil* the amoralist looks upon as the outstreaming of human instincts, in fact, as the good. He does not consider punishment as morally necessary but merely as a means of eradicating instincts of certain human beings which are harmful to others. According to the opinion of the amoralist, society does not punish for this reason but because it has "moral right" to expiate the guilt, and because it proves itself stronger than the individual who has instincts which are antagonistic to the whole. The power of society stands against the power of the individual. This is the natural connection between an "evil" action of the individual and the justification of society, leading to the punishment of the individual. It is the *will to power,* namely, the acting of these instincts present in the majority of human beings, which expresses itself in the administration of justice in society. Thus, each punishment is the victory of a majority over an individual. Should the individual be victorious over society, then his action must be considered *good,* and that of others, *evil.* The arbitrary *right* expresses only what society recognizes as the best basis of their will to power.

24.

Because Nietzsche sees in human action only an outstreaming of instincts, and these latter differ according to different people, it seems necessary to him that their actions also be different. For this reason, Nietzsche is a decided opponent of the democratic premise, equal rights and equal duties for all. Human beings are dissimilar; for this reason their rights and duties also must be dissimilar. The natural course of world history will always point out strong and weak, creative and uncreative human beings. And the strong will always be destined to determine the goals of the weak. Yes, still more: the strong will make use of the weak as the means toward a certain goal, that is, to serve as slaves. Nietzsche naturally does not speak about the "moral" right of the strong to keep slaves. "Moral" rights he does not acknowledge. He is simply of the opinion that the overcoming of the weak by the strong, which he considers as the principle of all life, must necessarily lead toward slavery.

It is also natural that those overcome will rebel against the overcomer. When this rebellion cannot express itself through a deed it will at least express itself in feeling, and the expression of this feeling is *revenge,* which dwells steadily in the hearts of those who in some way or other have been overcome by those more fortunately endowed. Nietzsche regards the modern social democratic movement as a streaming forth of this revenge. For him, the victory of this movement would be a raising of the deformed, poorly endowed to the disadvantage of those better equipped. Nietzsche strove for exactly the opposite: the cultivation of the strong, self-dominant personality. And he hates the urge to equalize everything and to allow the sovereign individuality to disappear in the ocean of universal mediocrity.

Not that each shall have the same and enjoy the same, says Nietzsche, but each should have and enjoy what he can attain by his own personal effort.

25.

What the human being is worth depends only upon the value of his instincts. By nothing else can the value of the human being be determined. One speaks about the worth of work, or the value of work, or that work shall ennoble the human being. But in itself work has absolutely no value. Only through the fact that it serves man does it gain a value. Only insofar as work presents itself as a natural consequence of human inclinations, is it worthy of the human being. He who makes himself the servant of work, lowers himself. Only the human being who is *unable* to determine his own worth for himself, tries to measure this worth by the greatness of his work, of his achievement. It is characteristic of the democratic bourgeoisie of modern times that in the evaluation of the human being they let themselves be guided by his work. Even Goethe is not free from this attitude. He lets his *Faust* find the full satisfaction in the consciousness of work well done.

26.

Art also has value, according to Nietzsche's opinion, only when it serves the life of the individual human being. And in this Nietzsche is a representative of the opinion of the strong personality, and rejects everything that the weak instincts express about art. All German aesthetes represent the point of view of the weak instincts. Art should represent the "infinite" in the "finite," the "eternal" in the "temporal," and the "idea" in the "reality." For Schelling, as an example, all sensual beauty is but a reflection of that *infinite* beauty which we can never perceive with our senses. The work of art is never there for the sake of itself, nor is beautiful through what it is, but only because it reflects the *idea* of the beautiful. The sense picture is only a means of expression, only the form for a *supersensible* content, and Hegel calls the beautiful, "the sense filled appearance of the *Idea*." Similar thoughts also can be found among other German aesthetes. For Nietzsche, art is a life-fostering element, and only when this is the case, has it justification. The one who cannot bear life as he directly perceives it, transforms it according to his requirements, and thereby creates a work of art. And what does the one who enjoys it demand from the work of art? He demands heightening of his joy of life, the strengthening of his life forces, satisfaction of his requirements, which reality does not do for him. But in the work of art, when his senses are directed toward the real, he will not see any reflection of the divine or of the super-earthy. Let us hear how Nietzsche describes the impression Bizet's *Carmen* made upon him: "I become a better man when Bizet speaks to me. Also a better musician, a better *listener*. Is it at all possible to listen still better? I continue to bury my ears beneath this music; I hear its wellsprings. It seems to me that I experience its development, its evolving. I tremble in face of dangers which accompany any daring adventure. I am delighted with happy fortunes for which Bizet is not responsible. And, strange! fundamentally I do not think about it, nor do I even know how much I ponder about it. For, meanwhile, entirely different thoughts run through my head. Has one noticed that music *frees* the spirit, gives wings to the thoughts, that one becomes more of a philosopher, the more one becomes a musician, that the grey heavens of abstraction are lighted by flashes of lightning, that the light is strong enough for all the tracery of things, the large problems near enough for grasping, and the world is seen as from a mountain? I have just defined philosophical pathos. And, inadvertently, *answers* fall into my lap, a small hail of ice and wisdom, of *solved* problems. Where am I? Bizet makes me fruitful. All good makes me fruitful. I have no other gratitude, I also have no other *measure* for that which is good." (*Case of Wagner*, ¶ 1.) Since Richard Wagner's music did not make such an impression upon him, Nietzsche rejected it: "My objections to Wagner's music are physiological objections. . . . As a fact, my *petit fait vrai* is that I no longer breathe easily when this music first begins to work upon me; that soon my *foot* becomes *angry* with it and revolts: it desires to beat, dance, march. It demands first of all from the music the pleasures which lie in *good* walking, striding dancing. But doesn't my stomach also protest? My heart? My circulation? Do not my intestines also grieve? Do I not become unknowingly hoarse? And so I ask myself, 'What does my entire body really *want* from this music?' I believe that it seeks levitation. It is as if all animal functions become accelerated through these light, bold, abandoned, self-sure rhythms; as if the brazen, leaden life would lose its weight through the golden tender flow of oily melodies. My melancholy heaviness could *rest* in the hide and seek and in the abysses of *perfection;* but for that I need music." (*Nietzsche contra Wagner*)

At the beginning of his literary career Nietzsche deceived himself about what his instincts demanded from art, and thus at that time he was a disciple of Wagner. He had allowed himself to be lead astray into idealism through the study of Schopenhauer's philosophy. He believed in idealism for a certain time, and conjured up before himself artistic needs, ideal needs. Only in the further course of his life did he notice that all idealism was exactly contrary to his impulses. Now he became more honest with himself. He expressed only what he himself felt. And this could only lead to the complete rejection of Wagner's music, which as a mark of Wagner's last working aim, assumed an ever more ascetic character, as mentioned above.

The aesthetes who demand that art make the ideal tangible, that it materialize the divine, in this field present an opinion similar to the philosophical nihilist in the field of knowledge and morality. In the objects of art they search for a beyond which, before the sense of reality, dissolves itself into a *nothingness*. There is also an *aesthetic nihilism*.

This stands in contrast to the aestheticism of the strong personality, which sees in art a reflection of reality, a higher reality, which man would rather enjoy than the commonplace.

27.

Nietzsche places two types of human beings opposite each other: the weak and the strong. The first type looks for knowledge as an objective fact, which should stream from the outer world into his spirit. He allows himself to have his good and evil dictated by an "eternal world will" or a "categorical imperative." He identifies each action as sin which is not determined by this world will, but only by the creative self-will, a sin which must entail a moral punishment. The weak would like to prescribe equal rights for all human beings, and to determine the worth of the human being according to an outer yardstick. He would finally see in art a reflection of the divine, a message from the beyond. The strong, on the contrary, sees in all knowledge an expression of the will to power. Through knowledge he attempts to make all things conceivable, and, as a consequence, to make them subject to himself. He knows that he himself is the creator of truth, and that no one but himself can create his good and his evil. He regards the actions of human beings as the consequences of natural impulses, and lets them count as natural events which are never regarded as sins and do not warrant a moral judgment. He looks for the value of a man in the efficiency of the latter's instincts. A human being with instincts of health, spirit, beauty, perseverance, nobility he values higher than one with instincts of weakness, ugliness or slavery. He values a work of art according to the degree to which it enhances his forces.

Nietzsche understands this latter type of man to be his superman. Until now, such supermen could come about only through the coalescing of accidental conditions. To make their development into the conscious goal of mankind is the intention of Zarathustra. Until now, one saw the goal of human development in various ideas. Here Nietzsche considers a change of perception to be necessary. "The more valuable type has been described often enough,

The Superman

but as a happy fortune, as an exception, never as *consciously willed*. Moreover, he specifically is most feared; until now he was almost *the* most terrible one; and out of the terror the reverse type was willed, bred, *achieved:* the domestic animal, the herd animal, the sick animal—man—the Christ." (*Antichrist*, ¶ 3.)

Zarathustra's wisdom is to teach about the superman, toward which that other type was only a transition.

Nietzsche calls this wisdom, *Dionysian*. It is wisdom which is not given to man from without; it is a self-created wisdom. The Dionysian wise one does not search; he creates. He does not stand as a spectator outside of the world he wishes to know; he becomes *one* with his knowledge. He does not search after a God; what he can still imagine to himself as divine is only himself as the creator of his own world. When this condition extends to all forces of the human organism, the result is the *Dionysian human being*, who cannot misunderstand a suggestion; he overlooks no sign of emotions; he has the highest level of understanding and divining instinct, just he possesses the art of communication in the highest degree. He enters into everything, into every emotion; he transforms himself continually. In contrast to the Dionysian wise one, stands the mere observer, who believes himself to be always outside his objects of knowledge, as an objective suffering spectator. The *Apollonian* stands opposite to the Dionysian human being. The Apollonian is he who, "above all, keeps the eye very active so that it receives the power of vision." Visions, pictures of things which stand beyond the reality of mankind: the Apollonian spirit strives for these, and not for that wisdom created by himself.

28.

The Apollonian wisdom has the character of *earnestness*. It feels the domination of the Beyond, which it only pictures, as a heavy weight, as an opposing power. The Apollonian wisdom is serious for it believes itself to be in possession of a message from the Beyond, even if this is only transmitted through pictures and visions. The Apollonian spirit wanders about, heavily laden with his knowledge, for he carries a burden which stems from another world. And he takes on the expression of dignity because, confronted with the annunciation of the infinite, all laughter must be stilled.

But this laughing is characteristic of the Dionysian spirit. The latter knows that all he calls wisdom is only his own wisdom, invented by him to make his life easier. This one thing alone shall be his wisdom: namely, a means which permits him to say Yes to life. To the Dionysian human being, the spirit of heaviness is repellent, because it does not lighten life, but oppresses it. The self-created wisdom is a merry wisdom, for he who creates his own burden, creates one which he can also carry easily. With this self-created wisdom, the Dionysian spirit moves lightly through the world like a dancer.

"But that I am good to wisdom, and often too good, is because she reminds me so very much of life itself. She has the eye of life, her laughter and even her golden fishing rod; how can I help it that the two are so alike? Into your

The Superman

eye I gazed recently, O Life: gold I saw flickering in your eyes of night! My heart stood still before such joy. A golden boat I saw flickering on the waters of night, a sinking, drinking, ever-winking, golden, rocking boat!

"Upon my foot, so wild to dance, you cast a glance, a laughing questioning, a melting, rocking glance. Twice only you shook your castanet with tiny hands. Thereupon, my foot rocked with urge to dance.

"My heels arched themselves, my toes listened to understand you. Indeed, the dancer carries his ear—in his toes!"
(*Zarathustra*—2nd and 3rd Parts. "The Dance Song.")

29.

Since the Dionysian spirit draws out of himself all impulses for his actions and obeys no external power, he is a *free* spirit. A free spirit follows only his own nature. Now of course in Nietzsche's works one speaks about instincts as the impulses of the free spirit. I believe that here under *one* name Nietzsche has collected a whole range of impulses requiring a consideration which goes more into individual differentiations. Nietzsche calls instincts those impulses for nourishment and self preservation present in animals, as well as the highest impulses of human nature, for example, the urge toward knowledge, the impulse to act according to moral standards, the drive to refresh oneself through works of art, and so on. Now, of course, all these impulses are forms of expression of one and the same fundamental force, but they do represent different levels in the development of this power. The moral instincts, for example, are a special level of instinct.

Even if it is only admitted that they are but higher forms of sensory instinct, nevertheless they do appear in a special form within man's existence. This shows itself in that it is possible for man to carry out actions which cannot be led back to sensory instincts directly, but only to those impulses which can be defined as higher forms of instinct. The human being himself creates impulses for his own actions, which are not to be derived from his own sensory impulses, but only from conscious thinking. He puts individual purposes before himself, but he puts these before himself *consciously,* and there is a great difference whether he follows an instinct which arose unconsciously and only afterward was taken into consciousness, or whether he follows a thought which he produced from the very beginning with full consciousness. When I eat because my impulse for nourishment drives me to it, this is something essentially different from my solving a mathematical problem. But the conceptual grasp of world phenomena presents a special form of general perceptability. It differentiates itself from mere sensory perception. For the human being, the higher forms of development of the life of instinct are just as natural as the lower. If both of them are not in harmony, then he is condemned to unfreedom. The case may be that a weak personality, with entirely healthy sense instincts, has but weak spiritual instincts. Then of course he will develop his own individuality in regard to the life of senses, but he will draw the thought impulses of his actions from tradition. Disharmony can develop between both worlds of impulses. The sense impulses press toward a living out of one's own personality; the spiritual impulses are fettered to outer authority. The spiritual life of such a personality will be tyrannized by the sensuous, the sensuous life by the spiritual instincts. This is because both powers do not belong together, and have not grown out of a single state of being. Therefore, to the really free personality belongs not only a soundly developed individualized life of sense impulses, but also the capacity to create for himself the thought impulses for life. Only that man is entirely *free* who can produce thoughts out of himself which can lead to action, and in my book, *Die Philosophie der Freiheit,* The Philosophy of Freedom, I have called the capacity to produce pure thought motives for action, "moral fantasy." Only the one who has this *moral fantasy* is really free, because the human being must act in accordance with *conscious* motives. And when he cannot produce the latter out of himself, then he must let himself be given them by outer authority or by tradition, which speaks to him in the form of the voice of conscience. A man who abandons himself merely to sensual instincts, acts *like an animal;* a human being who places his sensuous instincts under another's thoughts, acts *unfreely;* only the human being who creates for himself his own *moral* goals, acts in *freedom.* Moral fantasy is lacking in Nietzsche's teaching. The one who carries Nietzsche's thoughts to their conclusion must necessarily come to this insight. But in any case, it is an absolute necessity that this insight be added to Nietzsche's world conception. Otherwise one could always object to his conception thus: Indeed the Dionysian man is no slave to tradition or to the "will beyond," but he is *a slave of his own instincts.*

Nietzsche looked toward the original, essential personality of the human being. He tried to separate this essential personality from the cloak of the impersonal in which it had been veiled by a world conception hostile to reality. But he did not come to the point where he differentiated the levels of life within the personality itself. Therefore he underestimated the significance of consciousness for the human personality. "Consciousness is the last and most recent development of the organic, and consequently the least prepared and the weakest. Out of consciousness come innumerable errors, which bring it about that an animal, a human being, disintegrates earlier than otherwise would be necessary—collapses 'over his destiny,' as Homer says. If the preserved union of instincts were not so overwhelmingly powerful, if, on the whole it did not serve as a regulator, mankind would go to pieces because of their confused judgment, spinning fantasies with open eyes through their superficiality and gullibility. In short, just because of their consciousness, mankind must be destroyed," says Nietzsche *(Fröhliche Wissenschaft,* Joyful Science, ¶ 11.)

Indeed, this is entirely admitted, but it does not affect the truth that the human being is *free* only insofar as he can create *within his consciousness* thought motives for his actions.

But the contemplation of thought motives leads still further. It is a fact based upon experience, that these thought motives which the human being produces out of himself, nevertheless manifest an overall consistency to a certain degree in single individuals. Also, when the individual human being creates thoughts in complete freedom out of himself, these correspond in a certain way with the thoughts of other human beings. For this reason, the free person is justified in assuming that harmony in human society enters of its own accord when society consists of sovereign individualities. With this opinion he can confront the defender of unfreedom, who believes that the actions of a majority of human beings only accord with each other when they are guided by an external power toward a common goal. For this reason the free spirit is most certainly not a disciple of that opinion which would allow the animal instincts to reign in complete freedom, and hence would do away with all law and order. Moreover, he demands complete freedom for those who do not merely wish to follow their animal instincts, but who are able *to create* their own moral impulses, their own *good* and *evil*.

Only he who has not penetrated Nietzsche so far as to be able to form the ultimate conclusions of his world conception, granted that Nietzsche himself has not formed them, can see in him a human being who, "with a certain stylized pleasure, has found the courage to unveil what perhaps lurked hidden in some of the most sceret depths of the souls of flagrant criminal types." (Ludwig Stein, *Friedrich Nietzsches Weltanschauung und ihre Gefahren*, Friedrich Nietzsche's World Conception and its Dangers, p. 5.) Still today the average education of a German professor has not reached the point of being able to differentiate between the greatness of a personality and his small errors. Otherwise, one could not observe that such a professor's criticism is directed toward just these small errors. I believe that true education accepts the greatness of a personality and corrects small errors, or brings incompleted thoughts to conclusion.

iii NIETZSCHE'S PATH OF DEVELOPMENT

30.

I HAVE PRESENTED Nietzsche's opinion about supermen as they stand before us in his last writings; *Zarathustra* (1883-1884), *Jenseits von Gut und Böse*, Beyond Good and Evil (1886), *Genealogie der Moral*, Genealogy of Morals (1887), *Der Fall Wagner*, The Case of Wagner (1888), *Götzendämmerung*, The Twilight of Idols (1889). In the incomplete work, *Der Wille zur Macht*, The Will to Power, the first part of which appeared as *Antichrist* in the eighth volume of the *Complete Works*, these opinions have been given their most significant philosophical expression. From the text of the appendix to the above-mentioned volume, this becomes quite clear. The work is called 1. *The Antichrist*, attempt at a criticism of Christendom. 2. *The Free Spirit*, criticism of philosophy as a nihilistic movement. 3. *The Immoralist*, criticism of the most ominous type of ignorance: morality.

At the very beginning of his writing career, Nietzsche did not express his thoughts in their most characteristic form. At first he stood under the influence of German idealism, in the manner in which it was represented by Schopenhauer and Richard Wagner. This expresses itself in his first writings as Schopenhauer and Wagner formulas, but the one who can see through these formulations into the kernel of Nietzsche's thoughts, finds in these writings the same purposes and goals which come to expression in his later works.

One cannot speak of Nietzsche's development without being reminded of that freest thinker who was brought forth by mankind of the new age, namely, Max Stirner. It is a sad truth that this thinker, who fulfills in the most complete sense what Nietzsche requires of the superman, is known and respected by only a few. Already in the forties of the nineteenth century, he expressed Nietzsche's world conception. Of course he did not do this in such comfortable heart tones as did Nietzsche, but even more in crystal clear thoughts, beside which Nietzsche's aphorisms often appear like mere stammering.

What path might Nietzsche not have taken if, instead of Schopenhauer, his teacher had been Max Stirner! In Nietzsche's writing no influence of Stirner whatsoever is to be found. By his own effort, Nietzsche had to work his way out of German idealism to a Stirner-like world conception.

Like Nietzsche, Stirner is of the opinion that the motivating forces of human life can be looked for only in the single, *real* personality. He rejects all powers that wish to form and determine the individual personality from outside. He traces the course of world history and discovers

Nietzsche's Path of Development 123

the fundamental error of mankind to be that it does not place before itself the care and culture of the individual personality, but other impersonal goals and purposes instead. He sees the true liberation of mankind in that men refuse to grant to all such goals a higher reality, but merely use these goals as a means of their self-cultivation. The free human being determines his own purposes; he possesses his ideals; he does not allow himself to be possessed by them. The human being who does not rule over his ideals as a free personality, stands under the same influence as the insane person who suffers from fixed ideas. It is all the same for Stirner if a human being imagines himself to be "Emperor of China" or if "a comfortable bourgeois imagines it is his destiny to be a good Christian, a faithful Protestant, a loyal citizen, a virtuous human being, and so on. That is all one and the same 'fixed idea.' The one who has never attempted and dared not to be a good Christian, a faithful Protestant, or a virtuous human being, and so on, is *caught* and held captive in orthodoxy, virtuousness, etc."

One need read only a few sentences from Stirner's book, *Der Einzige und sein Eigentum,* The Individual and his very Own, to see how his conception is related to that of Nietzsche. I shall quote a few passages from this book which are specially indicative of Stirner's way of thinking:

"Pre-Christian and Christian times follow opposite goals. The former wish to idealize the real, the latter to realize the ideal. The former looks for the 'Holy Spirit,' the latter for the 'transfigured body.' For this reason, the former comes to insensitivity toward the real, with contempt for the world; the latter ends with the rejection of ideals, with 'contempt for the spirit.'

"As the stream of sanctification or purification penetrates through the old world (the washings, etc.), so the actual incorporation penetrates into the Christian; the God throws Himself into this world, becomes flesh and redeems it, that is, He fills it with Himself; but since He is 'the idea' or 'the spirit,' therefore in the end one (for example, Hegel) carries the idea into everything of this world and proves 'that the idea, that intellect, is within all things.' Him whom the heathen Stoics represented as 'the wise one,' compares with the 'human being' in today's culture, and each of them is a *bodiless* being. The *unreal* 'wise one,' this bodiless 'holy one,' of the stories becomes a real person, an *embodied* holy one, in the God *who has become flesh;* the unreal 'human being,' the bodiless I, becomes reality in the *embodied* I, in me.

"That the individual himself is a world history and possesses in the rest of world history his essential self, transcends the usual Christian thought. To the Christian, world history is made more important because it is the history of Christ or of 'man;' for the egotist, only *his own* history has value because he wishes to develop *himself,* not the idea of mankind; he does not wish to develop the divine plan, the intentions of divine providence, freedom, and so on. He does not regard himself as an instrument of the idea or as a vessel of God; he acknowledges no profession, does not claim to be here for the further development of mankind, and to add his little mite, but he lives his life in indifference to this, oblivious of how well or how ill mankind itself is faring. If it would not lead to the misunderstanding that a condition of nature was to be praised, one could recall Lenaus' *Drei Zigeuner,* Three Gypsies:—'What! am I in the world to realize ideas?'— To bring about the realization of the idea, 'State,' by doing my bit for citizenship, or by marriage, as husband and father, to bring into existence the idea of family? What matters such a profession to me? I live according to a profession as little as the flower grows and perfumes the air according to a profession.

"The ideal of 'the human being' is *realized* when the Christian concept is reversed in the sentence: 'I, this unique one, am the human being.' The conceptual question, 'What is man?' has then transposed itself into the personal one, 'Who is man?' By 'what,' one seeks for the concept in order to realize it; with 'who,' it is no longer a question at all, but the answer is immediately present within the questioner: the question answers itself.

"About God one says, 'Names do not name You.' That also is valid for the 'me:' no *concept* expresses the 'me;' nothing one gives as my being exhausts me; they are only names. Likewise, one says about God that He is perfect and has no obligation to strive for perfection. This also is valid for me alone.

"I am the possessor of my *own* power, and I am this when I know myself to be the *unique* one. Within this *unique* one the possessor of self returns again into his creative nothingness, out of which he was born. Each higher being above me, be it God or be it man, weakens the feeling of my uniqueness, and only fades before the sun of the consciousness: If I base my affairs upon myself, upon the individual, then they stand upon the temporal, upon the mortal creator who devours himself, and, I may say. 'I have based my affairs upon nothing.' "

This person dependent only upon himself, this possessor of creativity out of himself *alone,* is Nietzsche's *superman.*

31.

These Stirner thoughts would have been the suitable vessel into which Nietzsche could have poured his rich life of feeling; instead, he looked to Schopenhauer's world of concepts for the ladder upon which he could climb to his own world of thought.

Our entire world knowledge stems from *two* roots, according to Schopenhauer's opinion. It comes out of the life of reflection, and out of the awareness of will, namely, that which appears in us as doer. The "thing in itself" lies on the other side of the world of our reflections. For the reflection is only the effect which the "thing in itself" exercises upon my organ of knowledge. I know only the impressions which the things make upon me, not the things themselves. And these impressions only form my reflections. I know no sun and no earth, but only an eye which sees a sun, and a hand which touches the earth. Man knows only that, "The world which surrounds him is only there as reflection, that is, absolutely in relation to something else: the reflected, which is he himself." (Schopenhauer, *Welt als Wille und Vorstellung,* World as Will and Reflection, ¶. 1.) However, the human being does not

Nietzsche's Path of Development

merely reflect the world, but is also *active* within it; he becomes conscious of his own will, and he learns that what he feels within himself as *will* can be perceived from outside as movement of his body; that is, the human being becomes aware of his own acts twice: from within as *reflection,* and from outside as *will.* Schopenhauer concludes from this that it is the will itself which appears in the perceived body motion as reflection. And he asserts further that not only is the reflection of one's own body and movements based upon will, but that this is also the case behind all other reflections. The whole world then, in Schopenhauer's opinion, according to its very essence, is will, and appears to our intellect as reflection. This will, Schopenhauer asserts, is uniform in all things. Only our intellect causes us to perceive a multitude of differentiated things.

According to this point of view, the human being is connected with the uniform world being through this will. Inasmuch as man acts, the uniform, primordial will works within him. Man exists as a unique and special personality only in his own life of reflection; in essence he is identical with the uniform groundwork of the world.

If we assume that as he came to know Schopenhauer's philosophy, the thought of the superman already existed unconsciously, instinctively in Nietzsche, then this teaching of the will could only affect him sympathetically. In the human will Nietzsche found an element which allowed man to take part directly in the creation of the world-content. As the one who wills, man is not merely a spectator standing outside the world-content, who makes for himself pictures of reality, but he himself is a *creator.*

Within him reigns that divine power above which there is no other.

32.

Out of these viewpoints within Nietzsche the ideas of the *Apollonian* and of the *Dionysian* world conceptions form themselves. He turns these two upon the Greek life of art, letting them develop according to two roots, namely, out of an art of representation and out of an art of willing. When the reflecting human being idealizes his world of reflection and embodies his idealized reflections in works of art, then the *Apollonian art* arises. He lends the shine of the eternal to the individual objects of reflection, through the fact that he imbues them with *beauty*. But he remains standing within the world of reflection. The *Dionysian artist* tries not only to express beauty in his works of art, but he even imitates the creative working of the world will. In his own movements he tries to image the world spirit. He makes himself into a visible embodiment of the will. He himself becomes a work of art. "In singing and dancing, man expresses himself as a member of a higher community; he has forgotten the art of walking and speaking, and is about to fly, to dance up into the air. Out of his gestures this enchantment speaks." *Geburt der Tragödie,* Birth of Tragedy, ¶. 1.) In this condition man forgets himself, he no longer feels himself as an *individuum;* he lets the universal world will reign within him. In this way Nietzsche interprets the festivals which were given by the servants of Dionysus in honor of the latter. In the Dionysian servant Nietzsche sees the archetypal

Nietzsche's Path of Development

pictures of the Dionysian artist. Now he imagines that the oldest dramatic art of the Greeks came into existence for the reason that a higher union of the Dionysian with the Apollonian had taken place. In this way he explains the origin of the first Greek tragedy. He assumes that the tragedy arose out of the tragic chorus. The Dionysian human being becomes the spectator, the observer of a picture which represents himself. The *chorus* is the self-reflection of a Dionysically aroused human being, that is, the Dionysian human being sees his Dionysian stimulation reflected through an Apollonian work of art. The presentation of the Dionysian in the Apollonian picture is the primitive *tragedy*. The assumption of such a tragedy is that in its creator a living consciousness of the connection of man with the primordial powers of the world is present. Such a consciousness expresses itself in the myths. The mythological must be the object of the oldest tragedies. When, in the development of a people the moment arrives that the destructive intellect extinguishes the living feeling for myths, the death of the tragic is the necessary consequence.

33.

In the development of Greek culture, according to Nietzsche, this moment began with Socrates. Socrates was an enemy of all instinctive life which was bound up with powers of nature. He allowed only that to be valid which the intellect could prove in its thinking, that which was teachable. Through this, war was declared upon the myth, and Euripides, described by Nietzsche as the pupil of

Socrates, destroyed tragedy because his creating sprang no longer out of the Dionysian instinct, as did that of Aeschylus, but out of a critical intellect. Instead of the imitation of the movements of the world spirit's will, in Euripides is found the *intellectual* knitting together of individual events within the tragic action.

I do not ask for the historical justification of these ideas of Nietzsche. Because of them he was sharply attacked by a classical philologist. Nietzsche's description of Greek culture can be compared to the picture a man gives of a landscape which he observes from the summit of a mountain; it is a philological presentation of a description which a traveler could give who visits each single little spot. From the top of the mountain many a thing is distorted, according to the laws of optics.

34.

What comes into consideration here is the question: What task does Nietzsche place before himself in his *Geburt der Trägodie,* Birth of Tragedy? Nietzsche is of the opinion that the older Greeks well knew the sufferings of existence. "There is the old story that for a long time King Midas had chased the wise Silenus, the companion of Dionysus, without being able to catch him. When the latter had finally fallen into his hands, the king asked, 'What is the very best and the most excellent for the human being?' Then, rigid and immovable, the demon remained silent, until, forced by the king he finally broke out into shrill laughter with these words: 'Miserable temporal creature! Child of accident and misery! Why do you force me

Nietzsche's Path of Development 131

to tell you what is most profitable for you not to hear? The very best for you is entirely unattainable, namely, not to be born, not to exist, to be nothing. But the second best is for you to die soon.'" (*Geburt der Trägodie,* Birth of Tragedy, ¶ 3.) In this saying Nietzsche finds a fundamental feeling of the Greeks expressed. He considers it a superficiality when one presents the Greeks as a continually merry, childishly playful people. Out of the tragic feeling of the Greeks had to arise the impulse to create something whereby existence became bearable. They looked for justification of existence, and found this within the world of the Gods and in their art. Only through the counter image of the Olympic Gods and art could raw reality become bearable for the Greeks. The fundamental question in the *Geburt der Trägodie,* Birth of Tragedy, and for Nietzsche himself is, To what extent does Greek art foster life, and to what extent does it maintain life? Nietzsche's fundamental instinct in regard to art as a life-fostering power, already makes itself known in this first work.

35.

Still another fundamental instinct of Nietzsche's is to be observed in this work. It is his aversion toward the merely logical spirit, whose personality stands completely under the domination of his intellect. From this aversion stems Nietzsche's opinion that the *Socratic* spirit was the destroyer of Greek culture. Logic for Nietzsche is merely a form in which a person expresses himself. If no further modes of expression are added to this form, then the personality appears as a cripple, as an organism in which

132   Friedrich Nietzsche, Fighter for Freedom

the necessary organs are atrophied. Because in Kant's writings Nietzsche could discover only the pondering intellect, he called Kant a "mis-grown concept cripple." Only when logic is the means of expression of deeper fundamental instincts of a personality does Nietzsche grant it validity. Logic must be the outflow for the *super-logical* in a personality. Nietzsche always rejected the Socratic intellect. We read in the *Götzendämmerung*, Twilight of Idols, "With Socrates the Greek taste reverses in the direction of dialectic; what is it that really happens? Above all, an *aristocratic* taste is overthrown; the common people get the upper hand with dialectic. Before Socrates, the dialectic manners were rejected in good society; they were considered bad manners, they merely posed." (*Problem of Socrates*, ¶. 5.) If powerful fundamental instincts do not uphold a position, then the intellect which has to 'prove' sets in, and tries to support the matter by legal artifices.

36.

Nietzsche believed that in Richard Wagner he recognized a restorer of the Dionysian spirit. Out of this belief he wrote the fourth of his *Unzeitgemässen Betrachtungen*, Untimely Observations, *Richard Wagner in Bayreuth*, 1875. During this time he was still a strong believer in the interpretation of the Dionysian spirit which he had constructed for himself with the aid of Schopenhauer's philosophy. He still believed that reality was solely human reflection, and that beyond the world of reflection was the essence of things in the form of *primordial will*. And the *creative* Dionysian spirit had not yet become for him

Nietzsche's Path of Development

the human being creating out of himself, but was the human being forgetting himself and arising out of primordial willing. For him, Wagner's music-dramas were pictures of the ruling primordial will, created by one of those Dionysian spirits abandoned to this same primordial will. And since Schopenhauer saw in music an immediate image of the will, Nietzsche also believed that he should see in music the best means of expression for a Dionysian creative spirit. To Nietzsche, the *language* of civilized people appears *sick*. It can no longer be the simple expression of feelings, because words must gradually be used more and more to express the increasing intellectual conditioning of the human being. But, because of this, the meaning of words has become abstract, has become poor. They can no longer express what the Dionysian spirit feels, who creates out of this primordial will. The Dionysian spirit, therefore, is no longer able to express himself in the dramatic element in words. He must call upon other means of expression to help, above all, upon music, but also upon other arts. The Dionysian spirit becomes a *dithyrambic dramatist*. This concept "is so all encompassing that it includes at the same time, the dramatist, the poet, the musician" . . . "Regardless how one may imagine the development of the archetypal dramatist, in his maturity and completeness he is a figure without any hindrances whatsoever and without any gaps; he is the really free artist, who can do nothing but think in *all the arts* at the same time, the mediator and conciliator between apparently separate spheres, the reconstructor of a unity and totality of artistic possibilities which cannot be at all conjectured or inferred, but can be shown only through the deed." (*Richard Wagner in Bayreuth,* ¶ 7) Nietzsche revered Richard Wagner as a Dionysian spirit, and Richard Wagner can only be described as a Dionysian spirit as Nietzsche represented the latter in the above mentioned work. His instincts are turned toward the beyond; he wants to let the voice of the beyond ring forth in his music. I have already indicated that later Nietzsche found and could recognize those of his instincts which by their own nature were directed toward this world. He had originally misunderstood Wagner's art because he had misunderstood himself, because he had allowed his instincts to be tyrannized by Schopenhauer's philosophy. This subordination of his own instincts to a foreign spirit power appeared to him later like a sickness. He discovered that he had not listened to his instincts, and had allowed himself to be led astray by an opinion which was not in accord with his, that he had allowed an art to work upon these instincts which could only be to their disadvantage, and which finally had to make them ill.

37.

Nietzsche himself described the influence which Schopenhauer's philosophy, which was antagonistic to his basic impulses, had made upon him. He described it when he still believed in this philosophy, in his third *Unzeitgemässen Betrachtung, Schopenhauer als Erzieher,* Untimely Observations, Schopenhauer as Educator (1874) at a time when Nietzsche was looking for a teacher. The right teacher can only be one who works upon the pupil in such a way that the inmost kernel of the pupil's being develops out of the personality. Every human being is influenced by the cultural media of the time in which he lives. He takes into himself what the time has to offer in educational material. But the question is, how can he find himself in the midst of all that is pressing in upon him from outside; how can he spin out of himself what he, and *only* he, and nobody else can be. "The human being who does not wish to belong to the masses needs only to stop being comfortable with himself; he should follow his voice of conscience which calls to him, Be yourself! That is not innately you, that which you are now doing, now intending, now desiring! Thus speaks the human being to himself, who one day discovers that he has always been satisfied to take educational material into himself from outside." (*opus cit.*, ¶ 1.) Through the study of Schopenhauer's philosophy, Nietzsche found himself nevertheless, even if not yet in his most essential selfhood. Nietzsche strove unconsciously to express himself *simply* and *honestly*, according to his own basic impulses. Around him he found only people who expressed themselves in the educational formulas of their time, who hid their essential being behind these formulas. But in Schopenhauer Nietzsche discovered a human being who had the courage to make his personal feelings regarding the world into the content of his philosophy: "the hearty well being of the speaker" surrounded Nietzsche at the first reading of Schopenhauer's sentences. "Here is an harmonious, strengthening air; this is what we feel; here is a certain inimitable unreservedness and naturalness, as in those people who feel at home with themselves, and indeed are masters of a very rich home, in contrast to those writers who admire themselves most when they have been intellectual and whose writing thereby receives something restless and contrary to nature." "Schopenhauer speaks with himself, or, if one absolutely must imagine a listener, then one should imagine a son whom the father instructs. It is a hearty, rough, good-natured expressing of one's mind to a listener who listens with love." (*Schopenhauer* ¶ 2) What attracted Nietzsche to Schopenhauer was that he heard a human being speak who expressed his innermost instincts.

Nietzsche saw in Schopenhauer a *strong* personality who was not transformed through philosophy into a mere intellectual, but a personality who made use of logic merely to express the super-logic, the instinctive in himself. "His yearning for a stronger nature, for a healthier and simpler mankind, was *a yearning for himself,* and as soon as he had conquered his time within himself, then with astonished eyes, he had to see the genius within himself." (*Schopenhauer* ¶ 3.) Already in those days the striving after the idea of the superman who searches for himself as the meaning of his own existence was working in Nietzsche's mind, and such a searcher he found in Schopenhauer. In such human beings he saw the purpose, indeed, the only purpose of world existence; nature appeared to him to have reached a goal when she brought forth such a human being. Here "Nature, who never leaps, has made her only jump, and indeed a jump of joy, for she feels herself for the first time at the goal, where she comprehends that she must abandon having goals." (*Schopenhauer* ¶ 5) In this sentence lies the

Nietzsche's Path of Development 137

kernel of the conception of the superman. When he wrote this sentence Nietzsche wanted exactly the same thing that he later wanted from his Zarathustra, but he still lacked the power to express this desire in his own language. Already at the time when he wrote his Schopenhauer book, he saw in his conception of the superman, the fundamental idea of *culture*.

38.

In the development of the personal instincts of the single human being, Nietzsche sees the goal of all human development. What works contrary to this development appears to him as the fundamental sin against mankind. But there is something within the human being which rebels in a quite natural way against his free development. The human being does not allow himself to be led only by his impulses, which are always active within him at every single moment, but also by all that he has collected in his *memory*. The human being remembers his own experiences. He tries to create for himself a consciousness of the experiences of his nation, his tribe, yes, of all mankind through the course of history. Man is an *historical* being. The animals live unhistorically: they follow impulses which are active within them at one single moment. Man lets himself be determined through his past. When he wants to undertake something he asks himself, What have I or someone else already experienced with a similar undertaking? Through the recollection of an experience the stimulus for an action can be completely killed. From the observation of this fact, the question arises for Nietzsche:

To what extent does the human being's memory capacity benefit his life, and to what extent does it work to his disadvantage? The recollection which tries to encompass things which the human being himself has not experienced, lives within him as an historical sense, as study of the past. Nietzsche asks, To what extent does the historical sense foster life? He tries to give the answer to this question in his second *Unzeitgemässen Betrachtung, Von Nutzen und Nachteil der Historie für das Leben,* Untimely Observations, On the Advantage and Disadvantage of History for Life (1873). The occasion for this writing was Nietzsche's perception that the *historical sense* among his contemporaries, especially among the scholars, had become an outstanding characteristic. To probe deeply into the past: this type of study Nietzsche found praised everywhere. Only through knowledge of the past was man to gain the capacity to differentiate between what is possible and what is impossible for him; this confession of faith drummed itself into his ears. Only the one who knows how a nation has developed can estimate what is advantageous for its future; this cry Nietzsche heard. Yes, even the philosophers wished to think up nothing new, but would rather study the thoughts of their ancestors. This historical sense worked paralysingly upon *the creativity of the present.* In the one who, with every impuse that stirs within him, has to determine first to what end a similar impulse has led in the past, the forces are lamed before they have become active. "Imagine the extreme example of a human being who simply does not possess the power to forget, who is condemned to see a coming into being everywhere; such a man no longer would believe in his own being, he would no longer believe in himself; he would see everything diffusing in moving fragments, and would lose himself in this stream of becoming. . . . Forgetting is a part of all actions, just as not only light, but also darkness is a part of all organic life. A human being who would wish to feel only historically through and through, would be similar to the human being who is forced to do without sleep, or the animal who is compelled to live only by chewing the cud, over and over again." (*History*, ¶ 1) Nietzsche is of the opinion that the human being can stand only as much history as is in accordance with his creative forces. The strong personality carries out his intention *in spite of* the fact that he remembers the experiences of the past; yes, perhaps just because of the recollection of these experiences, he would experience a strengthening of his forces. But the forces of the weak person are erased by this historical sense. To determine the extent, and through that the boundary "where the past must be forgotten if it is not to become the grave-digger of the present, one would have to know exactly the extent of the *plastic forces* of a human being, of a nation, of a culture; I mean, that power *to grow out of oneself in a unique way*, to transform and to incorporate the past and the foreign." (*History* ¶. 1.)

Nietzsche is of the opinion that the historical should be cultivated only to the extent that it is necessary for the health of an individual, of a nation, or of a culture. What is important to him is "to learn more about making history of *life*." (*History* ¶. 1) He attributes to the human being the right to cultivate history in a way that produces, if possible, a fostering of the impulses of a certain moment, of the present. From this point of view he is an opponent of the other attitude toward history which seeks its salvation only in "historical objectivity," which wants only to see and relate what happened in the past "factually," which seeks only for the "pure, inconsequential" knowledge, or more clearly, "the truth from which nothing develops." (*History*, ¶ 6) Such an observation can come only from a *weak* personality, whose feelings do not move with the ebb and flow when it sees the stream of happenings pass by it. Such a personality "has become a re-echoing passivism, which through its resounding, reacts upon other similar *passiva*, until finally the entire air of an age is filled with a confused mass of whirring, delicate, related after-tones. (*History* ¶. 6) But that such a weak personality could re-experience the forces which had been active in the human being of the past, Nietzsche does not believe: "Yet it seems to me that in a certain way one hears only the overtones of each original and historical chief tone; the sturdiness and might of the original is no longer distinguishable from the spherically thin and pointed sound of the strings. While the original tone arouses us to deeds, tribulations, terrors, the latter lulls us to sleep and makes us weak enjoyers; it is as if one had arranged an heroic symphony for two flutes, and had intended it for the use of dreaming opium smokers." (*History*, ¶ 6) Only he can truly understand the past who is able to live powerfully in the present, who has strong instincts through which he can discern and understand the instincts of the ancestors.

He pays less attention to the factual than to what can be deduced from the facts. "It would be to imagine a writing of history which contained not the least drop of ordinary empirical truth, and yet could make the highest demands upon the predicate of objectivity." (*History*, ¶. 6) He would be the master of such historical writing who had searched everywhere among the historical personages and events for what lies hidden behind the merely factual. But to accomplish this he must lead a strong individual life, because one can observe instincts and impulses directly only within one's own person. "*Only out of the strongest power of the present may you interpret the past;* only when you apply the strongest exertion of your most noble traits of character will you divine what is worthy to be known and to be preserved from the past, and what is great. Like through like! Otherwise you draw what is past down to yourselves." "The experienced and thoughtful writes all history. The one who has not experienced something greater and higher than others also will not know how to interpret something great and high out of the past." (*History* ¶. 6)

In regard to the growing importance of the historic sense in the present, Nietzsche judges, "That the human being learn above all to live and to use history only *in the service of the life which has been experienced.*" (*History* ¶ 10) He wants above all things a *"teaching of health for life,"* and history should be cultivated only to the extent that it fosters such a teaching of health.

What is life-fostering in such an observation of history? This is the question Nietzsche asks in his *History*, and with this question he stands already at the place which he described in the above-mentioned sentence from *Jenseits von Gut und Böse*, Beyond Good and Evil, page 9.

39.

The soul mood of the bourgeois Philistine works especially strongly against the sound development of the basic personality. A Philistine is the opposite of a human being who finds his satisfactions in the free expression of his native capacities. The Philistine will grant validity to this expression only to the extent that it adapts to a certain average of human ability. As long as the Philistine remains within his boundaries, no objection is to be made against him. The one who wants to remain an average human being will have to settle this with himself. Among his contemporaries Nietzsche found those who wanted to make their narrow-minded soul mood the normal soul mood of all men; who regarded their narrow-mindedness as the only true humanity. Among these he counted David Friedrich Strauss, the aesthete, Friedrich Theodore Vischer, and others. He thinks Vischer, in a lecture which the latter held in memory of Holderlin, set aside this Philistine faith without conquering it. He sees this in these words: "He, (Holderlin) was one of those unarmed souls, he was the *Werther* of Greece, hopelessly in love; it was a life full of softness and yearning, but also strength and content was in his willing, and greatness, fullness, and life in his style, which reminds one here and there of Aeschylus. However, his spirit had too little hardness: it lacked humor as a weapon; *he could not tolerate it that one was*

Nietzsche's Path of Development 143

not a barbarian if one was a Philistine." (*David Strauss*, ¶. 2) The Philistine will not exactly discount the right to existence of the outstanding human beings, but he means that they will die because of reality, if they do not know how to come to terms with the adaptations which the average human being has made regarding his requirements. These adaptations are once and for all the only thing which is real, which is sensible, and into these the great human being must also fit himself. Out of this narrow-minded mood has David Strauss written his book, *Der alte und der neue Glaube,* The Old and the New Faith. Against this book, or rather, against the mood which comes to expression in this book, is directed the first of Nietzsche's *Unzeitgemässen Betrachtungen, David Strauss, der Bekenner und Schriftsteller,* Untimely Observations: David Strauss, the Adherer and Writer (1873). The impression of the newer natural scientific achievements upon the Philistine is of such a nature that he says, "The Christian point of view of an immortal heavenly life, along with all the other comforts of the Christian religion, has collapsed irretrievably." (*David Strauss*, ¶. 4) He will arrange his life on earth comfortably, according to the ideas of natural science; that is, so comfortably that it answers the purposes of the Philistine. Now the Philistine shows that one can be happy and satisfied despite the fact that one knows that no higher spirit reigns over the stars, but that only the bleak, insensate forces of nature rule over all world events. "During these last years we have taken active part in the great national war and the setting up of the German State, and we find ourselves elated in our inmost being by this unexpected, majestic turn of events concerning our heavily-tried nation. We further the understanding of these matters by historical studies which nowadays, through a series of attractive and popular historical books, is made simple for the layman as well; in addition, we try to broaden our knowledge of natural science, for which also there is no lack of generally understandable material; and finally, we discover in the writings of our great poets, in the performances of the works of our great musicians, a stimulation for spirit and soul, for fantasy and humor, which leaves nothing to be desired. Thus we live, thus we travel, full of joy." (Strauss, *Der alte und neue Glaube,* The Old and New Faith, ¶. 88)

The gospel of the most trivial enjoyment of life speaks from these words. Everything that goes beyond the trivial, the Philistine calls unsound. About the *Ninth Symphony* of Beethoven, Strauss says that this work is only popular with those for whom "the baroque stands as the talented, the formless as the noble" (*Der alte und neue Glaube,* The Old and New Faith, ¶. 109); about Schopenhauer, the Messiah of Philistinism knows enough to announce that for such an "unsound and unprofitable" philosophy as Schopenhauer's, one should waste no proofs, but quips and sallies alone are suitable. (*David Strauss,* ¶ 6) By *sound,* the Philistine means only what accords with the average education.

As the moral, archetypal commandment, Strauss presents this sentence: "All moral action is a self-determining of the individual according to the idea of species." (*Der alte und neue Glaube,* The Old and New Faith, ¶ 74) Nietzsche

Nietzsche's Path of Development 145

replies to this, "Translated into the explicit and comprehensible, it means only: Live as a human being and not as a monkey or a seal. This command, unfortunately, is completely useless and powerless, because in the concept, human being, the most manifold concepts are united beneath the same yoke; for example, the Patagonian and Magister Strauss; and because no one would dare to say with equal right, Live as a Patagonian, and, Live as Magister Strauss!" (*David Strauss*, ¶ 7)

It is an ideal, indeed, an ideal of the most lamentable kind, which Strauss wishes to set before men. And Nietzsche protests against it; he protests because in him a lively instinct cries out, Do not live like Magister Strauss, but live as is proper for you!

40.

Only in the writing, *Menschliches, Allzumenschliches,* Human, All-Too-Human, (1878), does Nietzsche appear to be free from the influence of Schopenhauer's way of thinking. He has given up looking for supernatural causes for natural events; he seeks natural proofs for understanding. Now he regards all human life as a kind of natural happening; in the human being he sees the highest *product* of *nature*. One lives "finally among human beings, and with one's self as in *nature*, without praise, without reproach, ambition, enjoying one's self in many things, as in a play, before which until now one had been full of fear. One would be *free* of the emphasis, and would no longer feel the goading of thoughts that one was not only nature or was more than nature . . . rather must a human being, from whom the usual fetters of life have fallen away to such an extent that he continues to live on, only to know ever more how to renounce much, Yes, almost everything upon which other human beings place value, without envy and discontent; for him, that most desirable condition, that free, fearless floating above human beings, customs, laws and the usual evaluation of matter, must *suffice.*" *Menschlices Allzumenschliches,* Human, All Too Human, I, ¶ 34. Nietzsche has already given up all faith in ideals; he sees in human action only consequences of natural causes, and in the recognition of these causes he finds his satisfaction. He discovers that one receives an erroneous idea of things when one sees in them merely what is illuminated by the light of idealistic knowledge. What lies in the shadow of things would escape one. Nietzsche now wants to learn to know not only the bright but also the shadow side of things. Out of this striving comes the work, *Der Wanderer und sein Schatten,* The Wanderer and his Shadow (1879). In this work he wishes to grasp the manifestations of life from all sides. In the best sense of the word, he has become a "philosopher of reality."

In his *Morgenröte,* Dawn (1881), he describes the moral process in the evolution of mankind as a natural event. Already in this writing he shows that there is no superearthly moral world order, no eternal law of good and evil, and that all morality has originated from the natural drives and instincts ruling within the human being. Now the way is cleared for Nietzsche's original journey. When no superhuman power can lay a binding obligation upon man, he is justified in giving his own creativity free reign.

Nietzsche's Path of Development 147

This knowledge is the motif of *Fröhliche Wissenschaft*, Joyful Wisdom (1882). No longer are fetters placed upon Nietzsche's "free" knowledge. He feels destined to create new values, having discovered the origin of the old, and having found that they are but human, not divine values. He now dares to throw away what goes against his instinct, and to substitute other things which are in accord with his impulses: "We, the new, the nameless, the incomprehensible, we firstlings of a yet untried future, we require for a new purpose a new means, namely a new health, a stronger, sharper, tougher, bolder, more audacious health than any previous states of health. The one whose soul bursts to experience the whole range of hitherto recognized values and wishes, and whose soul thirsts to sail around all shores of this ideal 'Mediterranean,' wants to know from his most personal adventures how it feels to be a conqueror and discoverer of ideals . . . he requires one thing above all, *health* . . . And now, after having been long on the way, we Argonauts of the ideal, more courageous perhaps than prudent, it will seem to us as recompense for it all that we have before us a still undiscovered land . . . After such outlooks and with such a craving in our conscience and consciousness, how can we allow ourselves to be satisfied with *the man of the present day?*" (*Fröhliche Wissenschaft*, Joyful Wisdom, ¶ 382)

41.

Out of the mood characterized in the sentences cited above, arose Nietzsche's picture of the *superman*. It is the counter-picture of the man of the present day; it is, above all, the counter-picture of Christ. In Christianity, the opposition to the cultivation of the *strong* life has become religion. (*Antichrist*, ¶ 5) The founder of this religion teaches that before God that is despicable which has value in the eyes of man. In the "Kingdom of God" Christ will find everything fulfilled which on earth appeared to be incomplete. Christianity is the religion which removes all care of earthly life from man; it is the religion of the weak, who would gladly have the commandment set before them, "Struggle not against evil, and suffer all tribulation," because they are not strong enough to withstand it. Christ has no understanding for the aristocratic personality, which wants to create its own power out of its own reality. He believes that the capacity for seeing the human realm would spoil the power of seeing the Kingdom of God. In addition, the more advanced Christians who no longer believe that they will resurrect at the end of time in their actual physical body in order to be either received into Paradise or thrown into Hell, these Christians dream about "divine providence," about a "supersensible" order of things. They also believe that man must raise himself above his merely terrestrial goals, and adapt himself to an ideal realm. They think that life has a purely spiritual background, and that it is only because of this that it has value. Christianity will not cultivate the instincts for health, for beauty, for growth, for symmetry, for perseverance, for accumulation of forces, but hatred against the intellect, against pride, courage, aristocracy, against self-confidence, against the freedom of the spirit, against the pleasures of the sense world, against the joys and bright-

Nietzsche's Path of Development 149

ness of reality, in which the human being lives. (*Antichrist,* ¶ 21) Christianity describes the natural as downright "trash." In the Christian God, a Being of the other world, that is, a *nothingness,* is deified; *the will to be nothing* is declared to be holy. (*Antichrist,* ¶. 18) For this reason, Nietzsche fights against Christianity in the first book of *Unwertung aller Werte,* Transvaluation of all Values. And in the second and third books he wanted to attack the philosophy and morality of the weak, who only feel themselves comfortable in the role of dependents. The species of human being whom Nietzsche wishes to see trained because he does not despise this life, but embraces this life with love and elevates it in order to believe that it should be lived only once, is "ardent for eternity," (*Zarathustra,* Third Part, The Seven Seals) and would like to have this life lived infinite times. Nietzsche lets his Zarathustra be "the teacher of the eternal return."

"Behold, we know . . . that all things eternally return, and ourselves with them, and that we have already existed times without number, and all things with us." (*Zarathustra,* Third Part, The Convalescent)

At present it seems impossible for me to have a definite opinion about what idea Nietzsche connected with the words "eternal return." It will be possible to say something more specific only when Nietzsche's notes for the incomplete parts of his *Willens zur Macht,* Will to Power, have been published in the second part of the complete edition of his works.

PART TWO

THE PSYCHOLOGY OF FRIEDRICH NIETZSCHE AS A PSYCHOPATHOLOGICAL PROBLEM

From the
Wiener Klinische Rundschau,
14th Year, No. 30, 1900

I

THESE LINES have not been written to add to the statements of the opponents of Friedrich Nietzsche, but with the intention to offer a contribution to the understanding of this man from a point of view which, no doubt, comes into consideration in passing judgment on his strange ways of thought. The thorough student of the world conception of Friedrich Nietzsche will come upon innumerable problems which can only be clarified through psychopathology. On the other hand, it should be of the greatest importance for psychiatry for students to occupy themselves with an important personality who has had an immeasurably great influence upon the culture of the age. In addition, this influence has an essentially different character from the effects philosophers usually have upon their pupils. For Nietzsche does not work upon his contemporaries through the logical power of his arguments. On the contrary, the wide dissemination of his concepts is to be traced to the same reasons which make it possible for zealots and fanatics to play their role in the world at all times.

A full clarification of the state of Friedrich Nietzsche's mind from the psychiatric point of view is not to be given here. Such an explanation is not possible today because a complete and true clinical picture of his sickness does not yet exist. Everything that has been presented concerning the history of his sickness, has the character of something fragmentary and contradictory. But the observation of Nietzsche's philosophy under the eye of psychopathology is entirely possible today. The real work of the psychiatrist would perhaps begin exactly where that of the psychologist, which is presented here, ceases. But this work is absolutely necessary for the complete solution of "the problem of Nietzsche." Only on the basis of such a psychopathological symptomatology will the psychiatrist be able to accomplish his task.

One quality which penetrates the entire creative activity of Nietzsche is the lack of a sense of objective truth. What science strove after as truth was fundamentally nonexistent for him. During the period shortly before his complete collapse into insanity, this lack increased to a formidable hatred of everything called logical reasoning. "Honest things, like honest people, do not carry their reasons in their hand. It is indecent to show all five fingers. What has to be proved first is worth little," he says in 1888, shortly before the *Götzendämmerung*, Twilight of Idols, was written, just before his illness (Volume VIII of the complete German edition of Nietzsche's Works, page 71). Because he lacked this sense of truth, he never fought

A Psychopathological Problem 155

through the battle which so many have to experience when, in their development they are forced to give up an acquired opinion. At his confirmation, when he was 17, he was completely a believer in God. Indeed, over three years later, as he left the Gymnasium in Schulpforta, he wrote, "To Him to Whom I owe most, I bring the firstfruits of my gratitude. What more can I sacrifice to Him than the warm feelings of my heart, which perceives His love more actively than ever: His love, which has allowed me to experience this most beautiful hour of my existence? May He, the true God, guard me henceforth!" (E. Foerster-Nietzsche, *Das Leben Friedrich Nietzsches*, The Life of Friedrich Nietzsche, Vol. I, page 194). Within a short time, a complete atheist developed out of this faithful believer in God, without an inner struggle. In his memoirs which he sketched in 1888, under the title *Ecce Homo*, he speaks about his inner struggles. "Religious difficulties," he says, "I do not know from experience. . . . God, immortality of the soul, salvation, life beyond, are pure concepts to which I have paid no attention, to which I have devoted no time, not even as a child; was I, perhaps, never sufficiently child-like for this? I absolutely do not know atheism as a result, still less as an event; it is understood by me only as instinct." (M. G. Conrad, *Ketzerblut*, page 182) It is indicative of Nietzsche's spiritual constitution that he asserts here that even as a child he had not given attention to the religious imaginations or ideas he mentions. From his biography which his sister has given us, we know that his classmates called him "the little pastor" because of his religious expressions. All this shows that he had overcome the religious convictions of his youth with greatest ease. The psychological process by which Nietzsche comes to the content of his conceptions is not that through which a human being passes who strives toward objective truth. One can already observe this in the way in which he arrives at his fundamental ideas in his first work, *Die Geburt der Tragödie aus dem Geiste der Musik*, The Birth of Tragedy Out of the Spirit of Music. Nietzsche assumes that two impulses lie at the basis of ancient Greek Art: the Apollonian and the Dionysian. Through the Apollonian impulse, the human being produces a beautiful image of the world, a task of peaceful observation. Through the Dionysian impulse the human being transfers himself into a condition of *intoxication;* he observes not only the world, but he permeates himself with the eternal forces of existence, and brings these to expression in his art. The *epic* style and sculpture are the results of Apollonian art. The lyric style, the musical work of art, are derived from the Dionysian impulse. The human being inclined to the latter impulse permeates himself with the world spirit, and brings its essence to manifestation in his artistic expressions. He himself becomes a work of art. "In song and in dance man expresses himself as a member of a higher community; he has forgotten how to walk and speak; he is about to take a dancing flight into the air. His very gestures bespeak enchantment." (*Geburt der Tragödie*, Birth of Tragedy, ¶ 1) In this Dionysian state the human being forgets himself; he feels that he no longer is an *individuum*, but rather an organ of the universal world will.

A Psychopathological Problem

In the festival games which were held in honor of the god Dionysus, Nietzsche sees the Dionysian expressions of the human spirit. He now imagines that the dramatic art of the Greeks arose from such games: that a higher union of the Dionysian with the Apollonian took place. In the oldest drama was created an Apollonian image of the human beings, aroused by the Dionysian impulse.

Nietzsche came to such ideas through Schopenhauer's philosophy. He simply translated the *Welt als Wille und Vorstellung,* World as Will and Idea, into the artistic. The world of reflection is not the real world; it is only a subjective image which our soul creates of things. According to Schopenhauer's opinion, through observation the human being absolutely does not arrive at the real essence of the world. The latter unveils itself to him in his willing. The art of reflection is the Apollonian, that of willing, the Dionysian. Nietzsche needed to go but one little step beyond Schopenhauer in order to arrive where he stood in the *Geburt der Tragödie,* The Birth of Tragedy. Schopenhauer himself had already assigned music to an exceptional position among the arts. He calls all other arts mere images of the will; he calls music a direct expression of the archetypal Will itself.

Now Schopenhauer never worked upon Nietzsche in such a way that one could say that the latter had become a dependent. In the book, *Schopenhauer als Erzieher,* Schopenhauer as Educator, Nietzsche describes the impression which he had received from the teaching of the pessimistic philosopher: "Schopenhauer talks with himself, or, if one absolutely must imagine a listener, then one imagines a son whom the father instructs. It is an honest, strong, kindly expression, before one who listens with love. We lack such writers. The powerful feeling of well-being of the speaker surrounds us at the first sound of his voice. It is an experience similar to entering a large forest; we breathe deeply, and suddenly feel ourselves exceptionally well. Here is an even, harmonious, strengthening air: this is what we feel. Here is a certain inimitable openness and naturalness, such as those people have who are at home in themselves; indeed, who are at home in a very rich house." This *aesthetic* impression is decisive in Nietzsche's relation to Schopenhauer. He was not at all concerned with the teaching itself. Among the notes which he had made at the time he had composed the pean of praise, *Schopenhauer als Erzieher,* Schopenhauer as Educator, one finds the following: "I am far from believing that I have rightly understood Schopenhauer, but rather, I have learned to understand myself a little better through Schopenhauer; this is why I owe him the greatest gratitude. But, all in all, it does not seem important to me that one goes to the depths of a philosopher and brings to light exactly what he has taught in the fullest sense of the word, and so on; such an understanding is least of all suited to human beings who are looking for a *philosophy of life,* not for a new *scholastic aptitude* for their *memory,* and in the end it remains improbable that such knowledge really can be found." (Nietzsche's Works, German Edition, 1896, Volume X, page 285)

Nietzsche, therefore, builds his ideas concerning the birth of tragedy upon the foundation of a philosophical structure of learning which he presents, whether or not he has rightly understood it. He does not search for logical, but mainly for aesthetic satisfaction.

A further evidence of his lack of a sense for truth is shown in his behavior during the composing of the book, *Richard Wagner in Bayreuth,* in the year 1876. At this time he not only wrote everything he could in praise of Wagner, but also many of the ideas *against* Wagner which he produced later in the *Fall Wagner,* The Case of Wagner. In *Richard Wagner in Bayreuth* he took only what could serve for the glorification of Richard Wagner and of his art; meanwhile, he kept the negative heretic judgment in his desk. Of course, no one would act in this manner who had a sense for objective truth. Nietzsche did not want to offer a true character sketch of Wagner, but rather to sing a song of praise for the master.

Most significant is Nietzsche's reaction to his meeting in 1876 with Paul Rée, who, when he studied a series of problems similar to those which interested Nietzsche, particularly the ethical, dealt with them in a strictly objective scientific spirit. This way of looking at things worked upon Nietzsche as a new revelation. However, this absolutely does not assume that Rée had a noticeable influence upon Nietzsche's world conception. He admired this pure searching for truth, which is entirely free of all romanticism. Malvida von Meysenbug, the intellectual author of *Memoiren einer Idealistin,* The Memoirs of an Idealist, in her recent book, *Der Lebensabend einer Idealistins,* Life Evening of an Idealist, speaks about Nietzsche's relation to Rée's mode of observation in the year 1876. At that time she belonged to the circle of people in Sorrento within which Nietzsche and Rée came closer to each other. "I saw from many conversations what a deep impression Rée's way of clarifying philosophical problems made upon Nietzsche." She relates a section of one of these conversations: "It may be," says Nietzsche, "the error of all religions to look for a transcendental unity behind appearance, and that may also be the error of philosophy and Schopenhauer's idea about the unity of the will to life. Philosophy may be just as gigantic an error as religion. The only worth-while and valid thing is science, which gradually adds stone upon stone in order to construct a safe building." This is clear speech. Nietzsche, who lacked the sense for objective truth in himself, almost idealized it when he encountered it in someone else. But the turning to objective science does not appear to him as a consequence. His way of working remains the same as before. Even now, the truth does not work upon him through its logical nature, but rather makes an aesthetic, pleasant impression upon him. In his two volumes, *Menschliches Allzumenschliches,* Human, All Too Human (1878), he sings one song of praise after another to objective science; but he himself absolutely does not apply the method of scientific knowledge. Indeed, he struggled along *his* way so that in 1881 he reached the point where he declared war against all truth.

During this time, Nietzsche made a statement by which he placed himself in conscious opposition to the points of view which natural science represents. This statement is his often-cited teaching about the "eternal return" of things. In Duhring's *Kursus der Philosophie,* Course of Philosophy, he found an argument which was to prove that an eternal repetition of the same world events is not compatible with the fundamental principles of mechanics. It was exactly this that led him to accept such an eternal, periodic repetition of the same world events. All that happens today has already occurred innumerable times, and is to recur innumerable times. During this period he also speaks about the pleasure it gave him to set up counter-arguments against universally accepted truths. "What is the *reaction of opinions?* When one opinion ceases to be interesting, one tries to give it new attractiveness by encouraging its counter-argument. But, usually the counter-argument misleads, and makes new advocates; meanwhile it has become more interesting." (Nietzsche's Works, German Edition, 1897, Volume XI, Page 65) And because he understands that his counter-opinion does not suit the old natural scientific truths, he makes the statement that these truths are not truths in themselves, but are errors which human beings have only accepted because they have proved useful in life. The fundamental truths of mechanics and natural science are really errors: this he wanted to emphasize in a work for which he sketched the outline in 1881. He tried all this only for the sake of the idea of the "eternal return." The logically compulsive force of truth was to be denied in order to be able to set up a counter-argument which runs contrary to the essence of this truth.

Nietzsche's struggle against truth gradually assumed still greater proportions. In his *Jenseits von Gut und*

Böse, Beyond Good and Evil, already in 1885 he asks whether or not truth has any value at all. "The will to truth which is to tempt us to many a hazardous enterprise, this famous truthfulness of which hitherto all philosophers have spoken with respect, what questions has this will to truth not laid before us? What strange, perplexing, questionable questions! It is already a long story, yet it seems as if it were hardly begun. . . . Granted that we want this truth, *why not rather untruth?*"

Such questions, of course, can also enter the most logical brain. The theory of knowledge must occupy itself with these questions. But for a real thinker, the natural consequence of the appearance of such questions is the search for the sources of human knowledge. A world of the most subtle philosophical problems begins for him. None of this is the case with Nietzsche. He enters into absolutely no relationship with those questions which have to do with logic. "I am still waiting for a philosophical *doctor* in the most exceptional sense of the word; one who pursues the problems of the entire health of a people, of a time, a race of humanity; such a doctor will have the courage to bring my suspicion to a head, and will dare to express the sentence, 'With all philosophers until now it is not at all a question of truth, but it is a question of something else, let us say, of health, future growth, power, life. . . . !" Thus Nietzsche wrote in the autumn of 1886 in the Preface to the second edition of *Fröhliche Wissenschaft,* Joyful Wisdom. One can observe that the inclination is present in Nietzsche to feel a contradition between life-usefulness, health, power, etc., and truth. Here, nat-

A Psychopathological Problem

ural feelings would not find an antithesis, but a harmony. In Nietzsche, the question of the value of truth does not appear as a need for theoretical knowledge, but rather as an outlet for his lack of objective sense for truth. This is shown grotesquely in a sentence which also appears in the Preface quoted above: "And in regard to our future, one will hardly find us again on the paths of those Egyptian youths who made the temples unsafe at night, embraced columns, and unveiled everything which for good reason had been kept hidden. They unveiled it, uncovered it, and wanted to bring it into bright light. No, this bad taste, this will for truth, for truth at any price, this madness of youth in their love for truth, is offensive to us." From this revulsion against truth stems Nietzsche's hatred for Socrates. The drive for objectivity of this latter thinker was something absolutely repulsive to him. This comes to expression in the strongest way in his *Götzendämmerung*, Twilight of Idols, 1888: "On the basis of his origin, Socrates belongs to the lowest people. Socrates was the mob. One knows, one can see for oneself, how ugly he was.... Socrates was a misunderstanding."

Let us compare the philosophical scepticism of other personalities with the struggle Nietzsche wages against truth. Ordinarily, at the bottom of this scepticism a sense for truth is really expressed. The drive for truth impels the philosophers to search for its value, its sources, its limits. In Nietzsche this drive does not exist, and the way he approaches these problems of knowledge is but the result of his erroneous sense of truth. It is understandable that in a talented personality such a lack comes to expression otherwise than in a subordinated way. However great the distance between Nietzsche and the psychopathically inferior people who lack a sense of truth in everyday life, qualitatively speaking, in him as in them one has to deal with the same psychological peculiarity which at least borders upon the pathological.

II

In Nietzsche's world of ideas is revealed an impulse to destruction, which in his judgment of certain points of view and convictions, allowed him to go far beyond what appears psychologically comprehensible in a critic. It is indicative that by far the greatest part of all Nietzsche has written is the result of this drive for destruction. In the *Geburt der Tragödie,* Birth of Tragedy, the entire Western cultural development from Socrates and Euripides to Schopenhauer and Richard Wagner, is presented as a path of error. The *Unzeitgemässen Betrachtungen,* Untimely Observations, on which he began work in 1873, was started with the decided intention "to sing off the entire scale" of his "enmities." Of the twenty observations planned, four were completed. Two of these are warlike writings which, in the most cruel manner, ferret out the weaknesses of the opponent Nietzsche attacks, or of the opinions unsympathetic to him, without bothering in the least about the relative justification of the one assailed. Of course, the other two are hymns of praise of two personalities; nevertheless, in 1888 Nietzsche not only retracted everything (in the *Fall Wagner,* Case of Wagner) he had said in glorification of Wagner in 1876, but Wag-

A Psychopathological Problem

ner's art, which he first praised as the salvation and rebirth of the entire Western culture, he later represented as the greatest danger for this culture. And he also writes about Schopenhauer in 1888, "In this sequence he has interpreted art, heroism, genius, beauty, the will for truth, the tragedy, as consequential appearance of negation or the need for negation of the 'will,' and this, with the exception of Christianity, is the greatest phychological forgery in history. More carefully considered, in this he is merely the heir to Christian interpretation, only that he still knew how to sanction what was rejected by Christianity and the great cultural facts of humanity in a Christian, that is, in a nihilistic sense." Therefore, even in face of things he once had admired, Nietzsche's sense of destruction, or drive toward destruction, does not rest. In the four writings which appeared from 1878 to 1882, the tendency to destroy established points of view outweighs all that Nietzsche himself brings forth as positive. For him it is of absolutely no consequence to search for new insights; he would much rather shake up those already existing. In 1888, he writes in his *Ecce Homo* about the work of destruction which he began in 1876 with his *Menschliches Allzumenschliches,* Human, All Too Human, "One error after another is calmly laid upon ice; the ideal is not refuted—*it freezes to death.* Here, for example, freezes the genius; in another corner further on, freezes 'the saint;' under a thick icicle freezes 'the hero;' at the end freezes 'the faith,' the so-called conviction; sympathy also cools off considerably. Almost everywhere freezes the 'thing in itself' . . . " " . . . Human, All Too

Human, with which I prepared for myself a very quick, sudden end to all dragged-in, higher, cheating, 'idealism,' 'beautiful feeling,' and other womanlinesses . . ." This drive for destruction incites Nietzsche to pursue with almost blind anger the victims upon whom he has thrown himself. He brings out judgments against an idea, against a personality whom he believes he must reject,—judgments which are not at all in relation to the reasons he offers for his rejection. The way he pursues opposing opinions does not differ in degree, but merely in manner from that in which typically argumentative people pursue their opponents. It is less a matter of the content of the judgment which Nietzsche brings forth. Often one can justify the content. But in those cases where doubtless he was justified to a certain degree, one will have to admit that the way he reached his judgments represents a distortion in a psychological sense. Only the fascination of his form of expression, only the artistic treatment of language can cast a veil of deception over the facts. But Nietzsche's intellectual lust for destruction becomes especially clear when one considers how few positive ideas he is able to bring against the points of view which he attacks. He makes the assumption that all of culture up to the present has brought about a completely false ideal of humanity; to this objectionable type of human being, he opposes his idea of the "superman." As an example of a superman there floats before him a real destroyer, Cesare Borgia. To imagine such a destroyer in an important historical role gave him real, spiritual pleasure. "I see before me the possibility of a perfect superearthly magic and charm of color; it appears to me that it shines in all its dreadfulness of refined beauty, that an art is at work, so divine, so divinely devilish, that one would search in vain for thousands upon thousands of years for a second such possibility. I see a drama so rich in sensuality, and at the same time so marvelously paradox, that all the deities in Olympus would have had occasion for immortal laughter—Cesare Borgia as Pope. . . . Does anyone understand me? Well, that would have been the victory for which I long today; with that Christianity was done away with." (Nietzsche's Works, German Edition, Volume VIII, page 311) How Nietzsche's sense for destruction outweighs his constructiveness shows itself in the disposition of his last work, in his *Umwertung aller Werte,* Transvaluation of All Values. Three-quarters of it were to be purely negative work. He offers a destruction of Christianity under the title *Der Antichrist,* The Antichrist; an annihilation of all present philosophies which he called a "nihilistic movement," under the title, *Der freie Geist,* The Free Spirit; and an annihilation of all previous moral concepts, in *The Immoralist.* He called these moral concepts "the most fateful form of ignorance." Only the last chapter announces something positive: *Dionysus, Philosophie der Ewigen Wiederkunft,* Philosophy of the Eternal Return (Nietzsche's Works, German Edition, 1897, Volume VIII, Appendix, page 3). He has been able to fill only this positive part of his philosophy with any substantial content.

Nietzsche does not shy away from the worst contradictions, if it is a question of destroying the arrangement of ideas of any cultural phenomena. When in 1888 in his *Antichrist* he is occupied with representing the harm of Christianity, he contrasts this with the older cultural manifestations: "The entire labor of the ancient culture is *in vain;* I have no words to express my feelings about something so monstrous . . . Why Greeks? Why Romans? All assumptions of a learned culture, all scientific *methods,* were already there; the great, the incomparable art of reading had already been established. This assumption of the tradition of culture, of the unity of knowledge, natural science in union with mathematics and mechanics, was already on the very best path; *the sense for the factual,* the ultimate and most valuable of all senses, had its schools; its old tradition had been established for hundreds of years! . . . and was not buried overnight by an event of nature . . . ! But it was brought to shame by clever, secretive, invisible anemic vampires! . . . One should just read any Christian agitator—St. Augustine, for example—to understand, to smell out, what unclean fellows have come to the surface." (Nietzsche's Works, Volume VIII, page 308). Nietzsche thoroughly despised the art of reading until the moment when he defended it in order to fight Christianity. Let us quote but *one* of his sentences about art: "I am thoroughly convinced that to have written one single line which deserves to be commented on by scholars, compensates for the service of the greatest critics. There is a deep modesty in the philologist. To correct texts is an entertaining task for scholars; it is a picture puzzle, but one should not regard it as something too important. It is too bad when antiquity speaks

A Psychopathological Problem 169

to us less clearly because a million words stand in the way!" (Nietzsche's Works, Volume X, page 341) And in 1882 Nietzsche's comments about the union of the factual sense with mathematics and mechanics, in his *Fröhliche Wissenschaft,* Joyful Wisdom: "That only that world interpretation is right which allows counting, calculating, weighing, seeing, touching, and nothing further, this alone is stupidity and naïvete, provided it is not insanity, or idiocy." "Shall we really allow our existence to be degraded to a slavish exercise in arithmetic, and a parlor game for mathematicians?" (Nietzsche's Works, Volume V, page 330)

III

We can clearly observe a certain *incoherence* in Nietzsche's ideas. Where only logical association of ideas would be in order, thought connections appear in him which rest merely upon external, accidental signs, for example, sound similarity in words, or metaphorical relationships which are completely inconsequential at a point where concepts are used. In one place in *Also Sprach Zarathustra,* Thus spake Zarathustra, where the man of the future is contrasted with the man of the present, we find this digression of fantasy: "Do like the wind when it rushes forth from its mountain caves: to its own piping will it dance; the seas tremble and leap under its footsteps. . . . That which giveth wings to asses, that which milketh those lionesses: praise be to that good, unruly spirit, which cometh like a hurricane unto all present and to all the populace . . . which is hostile to thistle-heads and puzzle-heads, and to all withered leaves and weeds: praised be this good, free spirit of the storm, which danceth upon fens and afflictions as upon meadows: which hateth the consumptive populace-dogs, and all the ill-constituted, sullen brood: praised be this spirit of all free spirits, the laughing storms, which bloweth dust into the eyes of these melanotic and melancholic ones!" (Nietzsche's Works, Volume VI, page 429) In the *Antichrist* is the following thought, in which the word "truth" in a quite external sense gives occasion for an idea-association at a most important point: "Must I still say that in the entire New Testament there is but one *single* figure which one must revere? Pilate, the Roman Governor. He does not convince himself into taking a Jewish affair seriously. One Jew more or less—what does it matter? . . . The noble scorn of a Roman, before whom a disgraceful misuse of the word "truth" has occurred, has enriched the New Testament with the single word which is *of value* . . . which is his criticism, his *annihilation* itself, 'What is truth?' . . . " (Nietzsche's Works, Volume VIII, page 280). It is absolutely a part of this class of incoherent association of ideas when, in *Jenseits von Gut und Böse,* Beyond Good and Evil, at the end of a discussion on the value of German culture, the following sentence which should have more value than a matter of style, appears: "It is artful of a people to make themselves be evaluated as deep, awkward, good-natured, honest, lacking in cleverness, or to *let* themselves be considered so, or, indeed it could be that they *are* deep! Finally, one should honor one's name; not for nothing is one called the deceiving nation. . . . "

A Psychopathological Problem

The more intimately one occupies oneself with Nietzsche's thought development, the more one comes to the conviction that everywhere there are digressions from that which is still explainable through psychology. The impulse to isolate himself, to separate himself from the outer world, lies deeply rooted in his spiritual organization. He expresses himself characteristically enough in his *Ecce Homo:* "I am gifted with an utterly uncanny instinct of cleanliness, so that I can ascertain physiologically, that is to say, that I can *smell* the proximity of, I may say, the innermost entrails of every human soul. . . . This sensitiveness has psychological antennae, with which I feel and handle every secret; the *hidden* filth at the root of many a human character, which may be the result of base blood, but which may be superficially overlaid by education, is revealed to me at first glance. If my observation has been correct, such people, unbearable to my sense of cleanliness, also become conscious on their part of the cautiousness resulting from my loathing; and this does not make them any more fragrant. . . . This is why social intercourse is no small trial to my patience; my humanity does *not* consist in the fact that I sympathize with the feelings of my fellows, but that I can *endure* that very sympathy. My humanity is a continual self-mastery. But I need *solitude,* that is to say, recovery, return to myself, the breathing of free, light, bracing air. . . . The *loathing* of mankind, of the 'rabble,' was always my greatest danger." (M. G. Conrad, *Ketzerblut,* page 183) Such impulses are fundamental in his teaching in *Jenseits von Gut und Böse,* Beyond Good and Evil, and in quite a number of his other ideas. He wants to educate a caste of prominent people who establish their life aims outside the realm of their complete arbitrariness. And the whole of history is only a means of training a few master natures, who make use of the remaining mass of humanity for their own personal purposes. "One completely misunderstands the predatory animal and the predatory human being (for example, Cesare Borgia), one misunderstands nature so long as one looks for something abnormal at the root of these healthiest of all tropical monsters and growths, or, indeed, searches for an inborn 'hell,' as almost all moralists have done up to now." (*Jenseits von Gut und Böse*, Beyond Good and Evil, p. 197) Nietzsche regards it as essential that a real artistocracy accept "with good conscience the sacrifice of innumerable human beings, who *for their sakes* had to be reduced to incomplete human beings, to slaves, to tools, and even had to be degraded." (*Ibid*, p. 258). From this comes Nietzsche's criticism of the social question, a criticism bordering upon narrow-mindedness. According to him, workers must remain cattle; they may not be trained to regard themselves as having any *purpose*. "In the most irresponsible and thoughtless way, one has destroyed the instincts which made it possible to be a worker, and to be one's self. One has made the worker militaristically efficient, one has given him the coalition right, the political vote; is it any wonder that today the worker fears his existence as a critical situation (morally expressed as *injustice*)? But what does one *want*? is asked again. If one wants a purpose, then one must also want the means; if

A Psychopathological Problem

one wants slaves, then one is a fool if one educates them to be masters." (Nietzsche's Works, Volume VIII, Page 153)

During the last phase of his creative activity, he placed the true personality in the very center of world events. "This book belongs to the very few; perhaps none of these is yet living. There may be those who understand my *Zarathustra;* how could I confuse myself with those for whom ears are growing already today? Only the day after tomorrow belongs to me. Some of my readers will be born posthumously . . . the conditions under which one understands me, and understands out of *necessity,* I know only too well. . . . New ears for new music. New eyes for the most distant. A new conscience for truths silent until now . . . Well! These alone are my readers, my true readers, my readers intended for me; what does the *rest* matter? The rest are mere humanity. One must surpass humanity in strength, in elevation of soul—through contempt. . . . " (Nietzsche's Works, Volume VIII, page 213) It is only an intensification of such ideas when Nietzsche finally identifies himself with Dionysus.

Nietzsche could think only in this way because in his isolation he lacked all reflection; for this reason his ideas were only nuances of what had worked itself to mastery of the spiritual life of the nineteenth century. He also lacked any understanding for the connections between his ideas and those of the scientific outlook of his age. What for others is the result of certain assumptions stands isolated in his system of ideas, and in this isolation grows to an intensity which gives entirely the character of *forced ideas* to his favorite points of view. His completely biological understanding of moral concepts bears this character. The ethical concepts should be nothing but expressions of physiological processes. "What is morality? A human being, a nation which has suffered a physiological change, senses this in a *community feeling,* and interprets it in the language of effects and *according to the degree* of their knowledge, without noticing that the seat of the change lies in the physical. It is as if someone were hungry and thought that he could satisfy his hunger with concepts and customs, with praise and with blame!" (Nietzsche's Works, German Edition, 1897, Volume XII, page 35) Such concepts, firmly established as the natural scientific world conception, work upon Nietzsche as forced ideas, and he does not speak about them with the security of the knower who is in the position to measure the extent of his ideas, but rather with the passion of the fanatic and the zealot. The idea of the survival of the fittest in the human "struggle for existence," quite familiar in the Darwinian literature of the last century, appears in Nietzsche as the idea of the "superman." The struggle against "the belief in the other world" which Nietzsche wages so passionately in his *Zarathustra,* is only another form of the struggle which the materialistic and monistic study of nature wages. What is fundamentally new in Nietzsche's ideas is only the tone of feeling in him, which is linked with his reflections. And the intensity of this tone of feeling is to be understood only when one agrees that these ideas, torn from their systematic connection, work upon him as forced ideas. Thus the frequent repetition of these reflections,

A Psychopathological Problem

the unmotivated manner in which certain thoughts make their appearance, are also to be explained. We can observe this complete lack of motivation particularly in his idea of the "eternal return" of all things and events. Like a comet this idea appears ever and again in his works during the period between 1882 and 1888. Nowhere does it appear in an inner connection with that which he brings forth otherwise. Little or nothing is produced to give it foundation. Nevertheless, it is held up everywhere like a gospel to call forth the deepest emotions of the whole human culture.

One cannot understand Nietzsche's spiritual constitution with the concepts of psychology; one must call upon psychopathology for help. With this assertion one does not wish to say anything against the quality of his creative genius. Least of all is a decision to be made concerning truth or error in his ideas themselves. Nietzsche's genius has absolutely nothing to do with this examination. The quality of genius appears in him through a pathological medium.

The genius of Friedrich Nietzsche is not to be explained from his sick constitution; Nietzsche was a genius *in spite of the fact* that he was ill. It is one thing to explain genius itself as a condition of a sick spirit, still another to understand the entire personality of a man of genius in relation to the morbid in his being. One can be a follower of Nietzsche's ideas and yet be of the opinion that the way Nietzsche discovers these ideas, brings them together, evaluates them, and presents them, is to be understood only through psychopathological concepts. One can admire his beautiful, great character, the strange physiognomy of his thinking, and yet admit that morbid factors enter into this character, into this physiognomy. The problem of Nietzsche is of particularly great interest, for the reason that a man of talent struggled for years with morbid elements, and because he was able to bring forth great ideas in a connection which is explainable through psychopathology alone. The expression of genius, not the genius itself, is to be explained in this way. Medicine will have much of importance to contribute to the understanding of the spiritual picture of Nietzsche. A light will also fall on the psychopathology of the masses when Nietzsche's spiritual nature is first understood. Of course, it is clear that it is not the *content* of Nietzsche's teachings that has brought him so many followers, but frequently the effect of his teaching is based precisely upon the unsound, unhealthy way he has presented his ideas. Nietzsche's ideas, first of all, were not a means whereby he understood the world and humanity, but rather a psychic discharge through which he wished to intoxicate himself; this is also true in many of his followers. Let us see how he himself describes the relationship of his ideas and his feelings, in his *Fröhliche Wissenschaft*, Joyous Wisdom. "Joyous Wisdom means the Saturnalia of a spirit who has patiently, strongly, coldly withstood frightful, long pressure, without being subservient, but without hope, and who is suddenly attacked by hope, the hope for health, the *intoxication* of convalescence. It is no wonder that much foolishness and nonsense comes to light thereby; that much arbitrary tenderness is wasted even upon

A Psychopathological Problem

problems which have a prickly hide and are not adapted to fondling and teasing. The entire book is really nothing but joyfulness after long denial and impotence; the rejoicing in a returning power, in a newly awakened faith . . . " (Nietzsche's Works, Volume V, page 3). It is not a question of truth in this book, but the discovery of thoughts which a sick spirit could find to be a healing remedy, a means of diversion for himself.

An intellect who wishes to grasp the evolution of the world and of humanity through his thoughts, needs the gift of imagination, which brings him to these thoughts, as well as self-discipline, self-criticism, through which these thoughts attain their meaning, their importance, their connection. This self-discipline does not exist to any great extent in Nietzsche. The ideas storm in upon him, without being kept in check by his self-criticism. There is no reciprocal relationship between his productivity and logic. No corresponding degree of critical thoughtfulness stands side by side with his intuition.

Just as it is justified to indicate the phychopathic origin of certain religious ideas and sects, it is also justified to test the personality of a human being on a basis which is not to be explained by the laws of psychology.

PART THREE

FRIEDRICH NIETZSCHE'S PERSONALITY AND PSYCHOTHERAPY

From the
Wiener Klinische Rundschau,
14th Year, No. 1, 1900

I.

"As the psychic processes act parallel with the brain stimulae, so physiological psychology goes side by side with brain physiology. Where the latter does not as yet offer sufficient knowledge, physiological psychology may make purely provisional investigation into psychic appearances, but always accompanied by the thought that for these psychic appearances the *possibility* of a parallelism with cerebral processes must also be proved." Even if one does not fully endorse this statement of Theodor Ziehen, (compare his *Leitfaden der Physiologischen Psychologie*, Guide to Physiological Psychology, page 2) one will have to admit that it has proved itself exceptionally fruitful for the methods of psychology. Under the influence of his point of view which he expresses, this science has attained truly scientific knowledge. But one must be quite clear about the significant light which the observation of the *pathological* soul appearances throws upon the connection between psychic appearances and the corresponding physiological processes. Pathological experimentation has rendered great service to psychology as well as to physiology. The abnormal facts of the soul life clarify the normal ones for us. But it must be especially important to follow abnormal manifestations into those realms where the soul activity intensifies to the point of the highest spiritual achievements.

A personality like Nietzsche offers special points of interest for such observation. A morbid kernel in his personality gave him occasion to return to the physiological groundwork of his reflections. He alternately sounded all notes from poetic diction to the highest points of conceptional abstraction. He expressed himself very sharply over the connection of his ideas with his physical condition. "In the year 1879 I completed my professorship in Basle, during the summer lived like a shadow in St. Moritz, and the next winter, the most sunless of my whole life, I existed like a shadow in Naumburg. This was my minimum. I reached the lowest point of vitality in my thirty-sixth year; I still lived, but without seeing three steps ahead of me. *Der Wanderer und sein Schatten,* The Wanderer and his Shadow, came to existence during this time. Without doubt, I then had an understanding for shadows. . . . The following winter, my first winter in Genoa, brought about that sweetening and spiritualization which is conditioned by an extreme poverty of blood and muscle, the *Morgenröte,* Dawn; the perfect clarity and joyousness, even exuberance of spirit, which the latter work reflects, is compatible with me, not only with the deepest physiological weakness, but also with an excess of painfulness. In the midst of my torment, which an uninterrupted three-day headache, together with the most wretched vomiting of slime brings with it, I possessed a dialectic clarity *par excellence,* and thought through things very cold-bloodedly, *for which, in a more healthy condition, I was not sufficiently a climber nor sufficiently crafty, nor sufficiently cold.* My readers know perhaps to what extent I consider dialectic as a symptom of decadence, for example, in the most famous instance: in the case of Socrates" (Compare M. G. Conrad, *Ketzerblut,* page 186, and Elizabeth Foerster Nietzsche, *The Life of Friedrich Nietzsche,* Volume II, page 328). (See also Nietzsche's Works, German Edition, 1911, Vol. XV. p. 9-12)

Nietzsche considered the change of his ways of thinking to be absolutely the result of the changeability of his physical condition. "A philosopher who has passed through many states of health, and will do so again and again, has also passed through many philosophies; he simply cannot do otherwise each time than to transpose his condition into a spiritual form and perspective; this art of transfiguration is his philosophy." (Nietzsche's Works, Volume V, page 8) In his recollections written in 1888, his *Ecce Homo,* Nietzsche tells how from his sickness he received the impulse to develop within himself an optimistic world conception: "For once, pay attention to this: the years of my lowest vitality were those when I ceased to be a pessimist; the instinct for self-reconstruction forbade me a philosophy of poverty and discouragement." (Elizabeth Foerster-Nietzsche, *The Life of Friedrich Nietzsche*, Volume II, page 338)

The contradictory in Nietzsche's world of ideas is understandable from this point of view. His physical nature moved in contrasts. "Provided one is a person, by necessity one also has the philosophy of a person; yet there is a substantial difference. In the one instance there are his deficiencies, which philosophize; in the other, his riches and his strength." (Nietzsche's Works, Volume V, page 5) In Nietzsche himself the two conditions alternated: one time the one, one time the other was dominant. As long as he was in full possession of his youthful forces, he considered the "pessimism of the nineteenth century as a symptom of a higher power of thought, a victorious fullness of life;" he considered the *tragic* knowledge, which he found in Schopenhauer, to be "the most beautiful luxury of our culture, its most costly, most aristocratic, most dangerous kind of waste, but always on the basis of its over-richness, as its *permitted* luxury." He could no longer see such a permitted luxury in the tragic knowledge, when the morbid in his life held the upper hand. For that reason, from now on, he creates for himself a philosophy of the greatest possible life-affirmation. Now he needed a world conception of "ego affirmation, ego glorification," a master morality; he needed the philosophy of "eternal return." "I shall return again with this sun, with this earth, with this eagle, with this serpent—not to a new life, or to a better life, or to a similar life: I shall come back eternally to this identical, this self-same life in the greatest and also in the smallest." "For the earth is a god's table, trembling with new, creative work and divine plans; Oh, how ardently I long for eternity and for the marriage ring of rings, the ring of the return!" *(Zarathustra,* Third Part)

The uncertain information we possess about Nietzsche's ancestry unfortunately makes it impossible to judge properly how much of Nietzsche's spiritual peculiarity is to be traced to inheritance. It is often incorrectly stated that his father died of a brain sickness. The latter contracted this illness through an accident only after Nietzsche's birth. However, it does not seem unimportant that Nietzsche himself points to a morbid element in his father. "My father died at thirty-six years; he was delicate, gracious and morbid, like a being destined only for a moment, or like a kind of recollection of life, rather than life itself." (M. G. Conrad, *Ketzerblut,* page 179) When Nietzsche speaks of the fact that within himself lived something decadent next to something healthy; he apparently considers that the former is derived from his father, the latter from his mother, who was a thoroughly sound woman.

We find in Nietzsche's soul life a series of traits bordering on the pathological, which remind one of Heinrich Heine and of Leopardi, who also are similar to him in other respects. Heine was tortured by gloomy melancholia from his youth, and suffered from dream-like conditions; later, out of the most pitiful physical constitution and increasing ill-health he knew how to create ideas which were not far removed from those of Nietzsche. Indeed, in Heine one finds almost a predecessor of Nietzsche, in the sense of the contrast between the Apollonian, or quietly observing attitude toward life, and the Dionysian, the dithyrambic life-affirmation. Heine's spiritual life also remains inexplicable from the psychological point of view if one does not take into consideration the pathological essence of his nature which he had inherited from his father, who was a weak personality, creeping through life like a shadow.

The similarities in the physiological characteristics of Leopardi and Nietzsche are especially remarkable. The same sensitivity toward weather and seasons, toward place and environment, are found in both. Leopardi feels the slightest change in the thermometer and barometer. He could create only during the summer; he traveled about, always looking for the most suitable location for his creative activity. Nietzsche expresses himself about such peculiarities of his nature in the following manner: "Now, after long practice, when I observe the effects of climatic and meteorological nature upon myself, as upon a very delicate and reliable instrument, and after a short journey, perhaps from Turin to Milan, calculate the change in the degree of humidity calculated physiologically in myself, then I look with horror at the *sinister* fact that my life until the last ten years, the most dangerous years, has always been spent in locations treacherous and absolutely *forbidden* to me. Naumburg, Schulpforta, Thuringia, in fact, Bonn, Liepzig, Basel, Venice,—all of them places of misfortune for my physiology. . . . " Connected with this unusual sensitivity in Leopardi as well as in Nietzsche, is a contempt for all altruistic feelings. Both of them had to overcome this in order to be able to tolerate mankind. From Nietzsche's own words one can see that his shyness in presence of strong impressions, of attractions which demand too much of his sensitivity, fill him with suspicion toward selfless impulses. He says: "I accuse those sympathetic people in that it is easy for them to lose the *modesty*, the *awe*, the *delicate feeling* for distances." For Leopardi also, it was certain that a bearable human being was very seldom found; he encountered misery with irony and bitterness, just as Nietzsche had adopted as one of his principles: "As first tenet of *our* love for mankind, the weak and misformed shall be destroyed. And one should even assist them in this." (Nietzsche's Works, Volume VIII, page 218) About life, Nietzsche said that it is "Essentially appropriation, injury, overwhelming of strangers and weaker ones, suppression, hardness, forcing upon others one's own forms, incorporation, and, in its least and mildest form, exploitation." (*Jenseits von Gut und Böse*, Beyond Good and Evil, p. 259) For Leopardi also, life is an unfeasible, frightful struggle, in which some trample others.

The extent to which both these thoughts play over into the pathological is shown in the completely rational way these men arrive at their ideas. They were not impelled to thoughts about the struggle for existence through logical reflection, as, for example, the national economist, Malthus, and the philosopher, Hobbes, or through careful observation as with Darwin, but through the high-strung sensitivity already mentioned, with the result that every external stimulus is regarded as a hostile attack, and is answered with violent rejection. One can prove this quite clearly in Nietzsche. In Darwin he finds the thought about the struggle for existence. He does not reject it, but he re-interprets it in such a way that it accords with his enhanced sensitivity: "But provided there is this struggle —and, in effect, it does happen—it comes about unfortunately in reverse from the way the Darwinian school wants it, as with them one may perhaps wish, namely, to the disadvantage of the strong, the privileged, the fortunate exceptions. The species does not grow in perfection; ever and again the weak become masters over the strong because they are in the majority, and because they are also cleverer. . . . Darwin has forgotten the spirit (that is English!) *the weak have more spirit* . . . the strong sacrifice the spirit" (Nietzsche's Works, Volume VIII, page 128).

Without doubt his heightened sensitivity and impulses impel him to a certain extent to direct his observations by choice upon his own personality. Entirely sound and harmonious natures, like Goethe, for example, find something questionable in far-reaching self-observation. In complete contrast to Nietzsche's way of reflection stands Goethe's point of view: "We must not interpret the significant saying, *Know thou thyself,* in an ascetic sense. With this by no means is meant the auto-gnosis of our modern hypochondriacs, humorists, and self-tormentors, but it means quite simply, take heed of yourself to a certain extent, observe yourself so that you become aware how you stand in relation to others like yourself, and in relation to the world. No psychological torments are necessary for this; every capable human being knows and experiences what this should mean; it is good advice, which is of the greatest practical advantage to everyone. . . . How can one learn to know oneself? We can never get to know each other through observations, but through action. Try to do your duty, and immediately you will know how things are with you." Now we know that Goethe also possessed a fine sensibility. But at the same time he possessed the necessary counter-balance, the capacity which, in regard to others, he himself described in the most direct way, in a conversation with Eckermann on the 20th of December, 1829: "The extraordinary" things that exceptional talents have achieved, "presupposes a very delicate organization, which makes them capable of rarer feelings. . . . Now such an organization, in conflict with the world and with the elements, is easily disturbed and injured: and the one who, like Voltaire, does not possess an extraordinary toughness, is easily subject to constant sickliness." This toughness is lacking in natures like Nietzsche and Leopardi. They would lose themselves completely in their impressions, in irritations, if they could not shut themselves off artistically against the outer world; indeed, if they could not oppose themselves to it in a hostile way. One compares this overcoming which Nietzsche required in his intercourse with mankind, with Goethe's pleasure in this intercourse, which he describes in these words: "Sociability was in my nature; thus I won co-workers for myself in my manifold undertakings, educated myself to be a co-worker with them, and so attained the good fortune to see myself live on, I in them and they in me."

II.

The most noticeable phenomenon in Nietzsche's spiritual life is the always latent, but at times clearly evident, schizophrenic quality of his ego-consciousness. That "two souls live, Alas, within my breast," bordered upon the pathological in him. He could not bring about the reconciliation between the "two souls." His polemics are hardly to be understood except from this point of view. He hardly ever really hits his opponent with his judgments. He first arranges what he wants to attack in the strangest way, and then struggles with the illusion, which is quite remote from reality. One understands this only when one considers that fundamentally he never fights against an external enemy, but against *himself*. And he fights in a more violent way when at another time he himself has stood at the point which he now regards with antagonism, or when at least this point of view played a definite role in his soul life. His campaign against Wagner is only a campaign against himself. He had half inadvertently united himself with Wagner at a time when he was thrown back and forth between contrary paths of ideas. He became the personal friend of Wagner. In his eyes Wagner grew to the immeasurable. He called him his "Jupiter," with whom from time to time he breathes, "a fruitful, rich, stirring life, quite different from and unheard of in more mediocre mortals! Therefore he stands there, deeply rooted in his own strength, his glance always over and above the ephemeral; eternal in the most beautiful sense." (E. Foerster-Nietzsche, *Das Leben Friedrich Nietzsches,* The Life of Friedrich Nietzsche, Volume II, page 16) Nietzsche was now developing a philosophy within himself, about which he could say to himself that it was entirely identical with Wagner's artistic tendencies and conception of life. He identifies himself completely with Wagner. He regards him as the first great renewer of the tragic culture which had experienced an important beginning in ancient Greece, but which was subordinated through the sophisticated, intellectual wisdom of Socrates, and through the one-sidedness of Plato, and in the age of the Renaissance had experienced a brief rejuvenation. Out of what he believed he recognized as Wagner's mission, Nietzsche formed the content of his own creating. But in his posthumous writings one can now see how he completely subordinates his second ego under the influence of Wagner. Among these writings are found dissertations from the time *before* and *during* his Wagner enthusiasm, which moved in directions completely opposite to his feelings and thinking. In spite of this he forms for himself an ideal picture of Wagner, which does not live in reality at all, but only in his fantasy. And in this ideal picture, his own ego vanishes completely. Later, in this ego appears a way of reflection which is the opposite of Wagner's method of conception. Now, in the true sense of the word, he becomes the most violent opponent of his own thought world. For he does not attack the Wagner of reality; he attacks the picture of Wagner which previously he had made for himself. His passion, his injustice, is only understandable when one realizes that he became so violent because he fought against something which had ruined him, according to his opinion, and which had taken him away from his own true path. If, like another contemporary of Wagner's, he had faced this objectively, perhaps he also might have become Wagner's opponent. But he would have faced the whole situation in a more quiet, calm attitude. It also comes to his consciousness that he does not wish to be freed from Wagner, but rather from his own "I" as it had developed itself at a certain time. He says: "To turn my back to Wagner was a tribulation for me; to like something again later was a victory for me. No one perhaps was more dangerously ingrown with this Wagner business, no one rebelled against it more strongly, no one rejoiced more to be free of it; it is a long story! Does one want a word for it? Were I a moralist, who knows what I should call it! Perhaps a *self-conquering*. What is it that a philosopher asks of himself at the beginning and at the end? To overcome his age in himself, to become 'timeless.' Against what does he have to wage his hardest struggle? With that in which he is exactly the child of his age. Well! I like Wagner as a child of this age; that is to say, a decadent: only that I comprehended it, only that I rebelled against it. The philosopher in me defended himself against it." (Nietzsche's Works, Volume VIII, page 1)

In the following words he more clearly describes his inner experience of the dividing of his ego and the immediate contrast of his world of thoughts: "He who attacks his time can only attack himself; what can he see otherwise, if not himself? So *in another, one can glorify only one's self.* Self-destruction, self-deification, self-contempt: that is our judging, our loving, our hating." (Nietzsche's Works, German Edition, 1897, Volume XI, page 92)

In the autumn of 1888, Niezsche cannot come to any agreement at all with himself about the content of his book, *Richard Wagner in Bayreuth,* other than that he tries to justify himself in that he did not mean Wagner at all, but himself. "A psychologist might add that what I had heard in Wagner's music in my youth had absolutely nothing to do with Wagner; that when I described the Dionysian music, I described that which *I* had heard; that instinctively I had to translate and transfigure everything into the new spirit which I bore within me. The proof for it, *as strong as proof can be,* is my book, *Wagner in Bayreuth;* in all psychologically decisive places *the question is only about me;* at will, one may put my name, or the name 'Zarathustra,' wherever the text mentions the name Wagner. The whole picture of the *dithyrambic* artist is the picture of the *pre-existentialist* poet of Zarathustra, drawn with profound depth and without touching the reality of Wagner for a single moment. Wagner himself had an idea of this, for he did not recognize himself in the book." (E. Foerster-Nietzsche, *Das Leben Friedrich Nietzsches,* The Life of Friedrich Nietzsche, Volume II, page 259)

Whenever Nietzsche fights, he almost always fights against himself. When, during the first period of his creative writing, he entered into active warfare against philology, it was the philologist in himself against whom he fought, this outstanding philologist, who, even before completing his doctorate, had already been appointed a Professor at the University. When, from 1876 onward, he began his struggle against ideals, he had his own idealism in view. And, at the end of his writing career, when he wrote his *Antichrist,* again unparalleled in violence, this was nothing but the secret Christian element in himself through which he was challenged. It had not been necessary for him to wage a special battle in himself in order to free himself from Christianity. But he was freed only in the intellect, in one side of his being; in his heart, in his world of emotions, he remained faithful to the Christian ideals in his practical life. He acted as the passionate opponent of one side of his own being. "One must have seen this doom near by; one must have been almost destroyed with it to understand that here is no joke. The skepticism of our natural scientists and physiologists is a joke in my eyes; they are lacking in passion for these things, in suffering for them." The extent to which Nietzsche felt the conflict within himself, and the extent to which he recognized himself as powerless to bring the different forces within him into a unity of consciousness, is shown at the end of a poem in the summer of 1888, that is, from the period shortly before the catastrophe. "Now, incarcerated between two nothingnesses, a question mark, a tired riddle, a riddle for *predatory birds* . . . they will 'free' you, they are already longing for your 'freeing,' they are already fluttering about you, you riddles, about you, the hanged one! . . . Oh Zarathustra! . . . *self-knower!* . . . *self-executioner!*" (Nietzsche's Works, Volume VIII, page 424)

This insecurity in regard to himself is also expressed in Nietzsche in that at the end of his career, he gives an absolutely new interpretation to his entire development. His world conception has one of its sources in ancient Greece. Everywhere in his writing one can point out what great influence the Greeks had upon him. He never tires of continually emphasizing the greatness of Greek culture. In 1875 he writes, "The Greeks are the only talented nation of world history; as learners they are very talented; they understand this best, and do not only know how to decorate and to refine the borrowed, as the Romans do. Genius makes all half-talented, tributary; thus the Persians themselves sent their messengers to the Greek oracle. How those Romans with their dry seriousness contrast with these talented Greeks!" (Nietzsche's Works, Volume X, page 352) And what beautiful words he found in 1873 for the first Greek philosophers: "Every nation is shamed when one points to such a wonderfully idealistic community of philosophers as those of the old Greek masters, Thales and Anaximander, Heraclitus, Parmenides, Anaxagoras, Empedocles, Democritus, and Socrates. All these people are hewn entirely from one stone. Between their thinking and their character strong necessity reigns. . . . Thus together they formed what Schopenhauer called a talent republic in contrast to the scholar republic; one giant calls to the other through the empty halls of the ages, and, undisturbed by the mischievous noisy ways of dwarfs who crawl beneath them, they continue the lofty conversation of spirits. . . . The first experience of philosophy on Greek soil, the sanction of the Seven Wise Ones, is at once a clear and unforgettable line in the picture of the Hellenic. Other nations have saints; the Greeks have Wise Ones. . . . The judgment of those philosophers about life and existence says altogether so much more than a modern opinion because they had life before them in luxuriant perfection, and because in them the feeling of the thinker did not go astray, as in us, in the conflict between the desire for freedom, beauty, largeness of life, and the impulse for truth, which asks only, What is life really worth?" (Nietzsche's Works, Volume VIII, page 7) This Greek wise one always stood before Nietzsche's eyes as an ideal. He tries to emulate him with the one side of his being, *but with the other side he denies him.* In the *Götzendämmering,* Twilight of Idols, 1888 (Nietzsche's Works, Volume VIII, page 167), after his description of what he wishes to owe to the Romans, we read, "To the Greeks I owe absolutely no strong kindred impressions; and, to say it straight out, they *can not* be for us what the Romans are. One does not *learn* from the Greeks; their way is foreign, it is also too liquid to work imperatively, 'classically.' Whoever would have learned writing from a Greek? Who would have learned it *without* the Romans! . . . The splendid, pliant corporality, and bold realism and immorality, which is part of the Hellenic, was a *necessity,* not something natural. It came only later; it was not there from the beginning. And from festivals and arts one wanted nothing more than to feel and act in a *buoyant* spirit; they are a means to glorify one's self, under certain circumstances, to create fear for one's self. . . . To judge the Greeks in the German manner, according to their philosophers, is to use, for example, the honorable gentlemen of the Socratic school for solving solutions which fundamentally are Hellenic! . . . The philosophers indeed are the decadents of Greece. . . ."

One will only gain full clarity concerning Nietzsche's arguments when one combines the fact that his philosophical thoughts rest upon self-observation, with the idea that this self is not an harmonious self, but is rather a self split apart. This splitting apart he also brought into his explanation of the world. In looking back upon himself he could say, "Do not we artists have to confess to ourselves that a weird difference exists in us, that our taste, and, on the other hand, our creative power, stand alone in a mysterious way, remain standing alone, and have a force of growth in themselves: I want to say, quite different degrees of tempos, old, young, ripe, dry, rotten? So that, for example, a musician is able to create things for life which *contradict* what his spoiled listener-ear, listener-heart, values, tastes, prefers; he doesn't even need to know about this contradiction!" (Nietzsche's Works, Volume V, page 323) This is an explanation of the nature of an artist, formed according to Nietzsche's own being. We encounter something similar in him in all his writings.

There is no doubt that in many cases one goes too far when one connects manifestations of the soul-life with pathological concepts; in a personality like Nietzsche's the world-conception finds full clarification only through such a connection. Useful as it might be in many ways to cling to the sentence of Dilthey's *Einbildungskraft und Wahnsinn,* Powers of Conceit and Illusion, (Leipzig, 1886), "The genius is no pathological manifestation, but the sound perfect human being," just as wrong might it be to reject dogmatically such observations about Nietzsche as have been presented here.

PART FOUR

THE PERSONALITY OF
FRIEDRICH NIETZSCHE
(A Memorial Address)

*A Memorial Address Given in Berlin,
on September 13, 1900*

It is strange that with the infatuation for Nietzsche in our day, someone must appear whose feelings, no less than those of many others, are drawn to the particular personality, and yet who, in spite of this, must constantly keep before him the deep contradictions which exist between this type of spirit, and the ideas and feelings of those who represent themselves as adherents of his world conception. Such a one who stands apart must, above all, beware of the contrast between the relationship of those contemporaries to Nietzsche a decade ago as the night of madness broke over the "fighter against his time" and what existed when death took him from us on the 25th of August, 1900. It seems as if the complete opposite has happened from what Nietzsche prophesied in regard to his effect on his contemporaries in the last days of his creative work. The first part of his book, in which he tried to recoin the values of thousands of years, his *Antichrist*, lay completed at the onset of his illness. He begins with the words, "This book belongs to the very few; perhaps not even one of these is yet living. There may be those who understand my *Zarathustra;* how could I confuse myself with those for whom ears are growing already today? Only the day after tomorrow belongs to me. Some of my readers will be born posthumously." At his death it seemed as if the "day after tomorrow" had already come. One must call into this apparent "day after tomorrow" the words of *Zarathustra:* "You say you believe in Zarathustra? But of what importance is Zarathustra? You are my believers, but of what importance are all believers? Now I exhort you to lose me and to find yourselves; and only when you have denied me will I return to you." Who would dare to say whether Nietzsche, were he to live today in fresh creativity, would look with greater pleasure upon those who revere him with doubts, or upon others? But it must be permitted, especially today, to look back, beyond these present-day admirers, to the time when he felt himself alone and misunderstood in the midst of the spiritual life surrounding him, when some people lived who felt it blasphemous to be called his "believers," because he appeared to them to be a spirit whom one could not encounter importunately with a "yes" or "no," but like an earthquake in the realm of the spirit, which stirs up questions for which premature answers can only be like unripe fruits. But ten years ago, more moving than the news of his death today, two pieces of news which followed closely upon each other, came to the "ears" which had "grown" for the Nietzsche admirers of that time. The first concerned the cycle of lectures which Georg Brandes had held about the world conception of Nietzsche at the Uni-

The Personality of Friedrich Nietzsche

versity of Copenhagen in the year 1888. Nietzsche felt this recognition to be one which had come forth from "single ones" which were "born posthumously." He felt himself jerked out of his loneliness in a way which was in harmony with *his* spirit. He did not want to be *evaluated;* he wanted to be "described," characterized. And soon upon this news followed the report that his mind, torn from its loneliness, had succumbed to the frightful destiny of spiritual darkness.

And, while he himself could no longer contribute, his contemporaries had the leisure to sharpen the outlines of his picture. Through the observation of his personality, the picture of the time could imprint itself ever more clearly for them; the picture of the time, from which his spirit rises like a Böcklin figure. The worlds of his soul ideals could be illuminated by the light which the spirit-stars of the second half of the nineteenth century cast upon them. In full clarity stood the points in which he was truly great. But these also overshadowed the reason why he had to wander in loneliness. The nature of his being led him over heights of spirit life. He stepped forth like one to whom only the essentials of mankind's development are of concern. But this essential touched him as much as others are touched in their soul by only the most intimate situations. Just as the souls of others are burdened directly by only the most immediate personal experiences, so the great questions of culture, the mighty needs for knowledge of his age, decisively passed through his soul. What permeated only the heads of many of his contemporaries, became for him a personal affair of the heart.

Greek culture, Schopenhauer's world conception, Wagner's music dramas, the knowledge of the more recent natural science, aroused in him such personal, deep feelings as would have been aroused in others only by the experiences of a strong, passionate love. What the entire age lived through in hopes and doubts, in temptations and joys of knowledge, Nietzsche experienced in his special way on his lonesome heights. He found no new ideas; but he suffered and rejoiced in the ideas of his time in a way different from that of his contemporaries. It was their task to give birth to the ideas; before him arose the difficult question, *How can one live with these ideas?*

His educational path had made Nietzsche a philologist. He had penetrated so deeply into the world of Greek spiritual culture that his teacher, Ritschl, could recommend him with these words to the University of Basel, which engaged the young scholar before he had taken his doctorate: Friedrich Nietzsche is a genius and is able to do whatever he puts his mind to. He may well have achieved excellent results in the sense of the requirements made of philologists. But his relationship to Greek culture was not only that of a philologist. He did not live in ancient Greece in thought alone; with his whole heart he was deeply engrossed in Greek thinking and feeling. The bearers of Greek culture did not remain the object of his studies; they became his personal friends. During the first period of his teaching activity in Basel, he worked out a book about the philosophers of the tragic age before Socrates. It was published among his posthumus works. He does not write like a scholar about Thales, Heraclitus and Parmenides; he converses with these figures of antiquity as with personalities with whom his heart is closely connected. The passion which he feels for them makes him a stranger to the Western culture, which according to his feelings, since Socrates has taken paths other than those of ancient times. Socrates was Nietzsche's enemy because he had dulled the great tragic fundamental moods of his predecessors. The instructive mind of Socrates strove toward an understanding of reality. He desired reconciliation with life through virtue. But there is nothing, according to Nietzsche, which can degrade mankind more than the acceptance of life as it is. Life cannot reconcile itself with itself; man can only bear this life if he *creates over and above* it. Before Socrates, the Greeks understood this. Nietzsche believed that he found their fundamental mood expressed in these words which, according to legend, the wise Silenus, the companion of Dionysus, gave as answer to the question, What is best for mankind: "Miserable creation of a moment, children of accident and travail, why do you force me to tell you what is not the most profitable for you to hear? What is the very best for you is not attainable by you; that is, not to be born, not to exist, to be nothing. But the second best for you is to die soon." Ancient Greek art and wisdom sought consolation in the face of life. The servants of Dionysus did not wish to belong to this community of life, but rather to a higher one. For Nietzsche this was expressed in their culture. "In song and dance, the human being expresses himself as a member of a higher community; he has forgotten how to walk and how to speak, and he is about to fly, to dance into the air." There are two paths for man which lead him over and above existence; in a blessed enchantment, as if in an opium dream, he can forget existence and, "singing and dancing," feel himself at one with a universal soul; or he can look for his satisfaction in an ideal picture of reality as if in a dream which flutters gently above existence. Nietzsche characterizes these two paths as the Dionysian and the Apollonian soul conditions. But the more recent culture since Socrates has looked for reconciliation with existence, and thereby has lowered the value of mankind. It is no wonder that with such feelings, Nietzsche felt lonely in this more recent culture.

Two personalities seemed to pull him out of this state of loneliness. On his life path he encountered Schopenhauer's conception of the worthlessness of existence, and Richard Wagner. The position he took in relation to these two clearly illuminated the being of his spirit. Toward Schopenhauer he felt a devotion more intimate than can be imagined. And yet Schopenhauer's teachings remained almost without importance for him. The wise one from Frankfurt had innumerable disciples who accepted faithfully what he had to say. But Nietzsche never was one of these believers. At the same time that he sent his pean of praise, *Schopenhauer als Erzieher,* Schopenhauer as Educator, into the world, he wrote secretly for himself his serious doubts about the philosopher's ideas. He did not look up to him as to a teacher; he loved him like a father. He felt the heroic quality of his thoughts even when he did not agree with them. His relationship to Schopenhauer was too intimate to necessitate an external faith in him or an outer confession. He loved his "educator" so much that he attributed his own thoughts to him in order to be able to revere them in another. He did not want to agree with a personality in his thoughts; he wanted to *live* in friendship with another. This desire also attracted him to Richard Wagner. What then were all those figures of pre-Socratic Greek culture with whom he had wished to live in friendship? Indeed, they were mere shadows from a far distant past. And Nietzsche aspired to life, to the direct friendship of tragic human beings. Greek culture remained dead and abstract for him, despite all the life his fantasy tried to breathe into it. The Greek intellectual heroes remained for him a *yearning;* for him Richard Wagner was a *fulfillment* which tried to re-awaken the old world of Greece within his personality, his art, his world conception. Nietzsche spent most glorious days when from Basel he was allowed to visit the Wagner couple on their Triebschen estate. What the philologist had looked for in spirit, to breathe Greek air, he believed he found here in reality. He could find a *personal* relationship to a world which previously he had sought in ideas. He could *experience* intimately what he could otherwise only have conjured before himself in thought. To him the Triebschen idyll was like home. How descriptive are the words with which he describes his feelings in regard to Wagner: "A fruitful, rich, stirring life, quite different and unheard of in more mediocre mortals! For this reason he stands there rooted deeply in his own strength, with his gaze over and above all that is ephemeral; eternal in the most beautiful sense."

In Richard Wagner's personality Nietzsche believed he had the higher worlds, which could make life as bearable for him as he imagined it to be in the sense of the ancient Greek world conception. But precisely here did he not commit the greatest error in *his* sense? Indeed he sought in *life* for what, according to his assumptions, life could not offer. He wanted to be *above* life; and with all his strength he threw himself into the life that Wagner lived. For this reason it is understandable that his greatest experience had to be his deepest disappointment at the same time. To be able to find in Wagner what he was searching for, he had first to magnify the true personality of Wagner to an ideal picture. What Wagner could never be, Nietzsche had made out of him. He did not see and revere the true Wagner; he revered his image, which towered far above reality. Then when Wagner had achieved what he aspired, when he had reached his goal, Nietzsche felt the disharmony between *his* impression and the true Wagner. And he separated from Wagner. But only he interprets this separation psychologically correctly who recognizes that Nietzsche did not separate from the true Wagner, because he never was his follower; he only saw his deception clearly. What he had looked for in Wagner, he could never find in him because that had nothing to do with Wagner; it had to be freed from all reality as a higher world. Then Nietzsche later characterized the necessity of his apparent separation from Wagner. He says that what in his younger years he had heard in Wagner's music, had absolutely nothing to do with Wagner. "When I described the Dionysian music, I described what *I* had heard; instinctively I had to translate and transfigure everything into the new spirit which I bore within me. The proof of this, as strong as proof as can be, is my book, *Wagner in Bayreuth;* in all psychologically decisive places one can place my name, or the name *Zarathustra* wherever the text uses the name Wagner. The complete picture of the dithyrambic artist is the picture of the pre-existentialist poet of *Zarathustra,* drawn with profound depth, and *without really touching the reality of Wagner for a single moment.* Wagner himself had an idea of this; he did not recognize himself in the book."

In *Zarathustra* Nietzsche sketches the world for which he had searched in vain in Wagner, separated from all reality. He placed his *Zarathustra* ideal in a different relationship to reality than his own earlier ideals. He had had bad experiences in his direct turning away from existence. He must have done injustice to this existence, and for this reason it had avenged itself so bitterly against him; this idea gained the upper hand within him more and more. The disappointment which his idealism had caused him, drove him into a hostile mood toward all idealism. During the time following his separation from Wagner, his works become accusations against ideals. "One error after another is placed upon ice; the ideal is not refuted—it *freezes to death."* Thus in 1888 he expresses himself about the goal of his book which had appeared in 1878, *Menschliches, Allzumenschliches,* Human, All Too Human. After this Nietzsche looks for refuge in reality; he deepens himself in the more recent natural science, in order that through it he can gain a true guide to reality. All worlds beyond this world, which lead human beings away from reality, now become abominable, remote worlds for him, conceived out of the fantasy of weak human beings, who do not have sufficient strength to find their satisfaction in immediate, fresh existence. Natural science has placed the human being at the end of a purely natural evolution. Through the fact that the latter has conceived the human being out of itself, all that is below him has taken on a higher meaning. Therefore, man should not deny its significance and wish to make himself an image of something beyond this world. He should understand that he is not the meaning of a super-earthly power, but the "meaning of this earth." What he wishes to attain *above* what exists, he should not strive for in enmity against what exists. Nietzsche looks within reality itself for the germ of the higher, which is to make reality bearable. Man should not strive toward a divine being; out of his reality he should bring forth a higher way of existence. This reality extends over and above itself. Humanity has the possibility to become superhumanity. Evolution has always been. The human being should also work at evolution. The laws of evolution are greater, more comprehensive than all that has already been developed. One should not only look upon that which exists, but one must go back to primeval forces which have engendered the real. An ancient world conception questioned how "good and evil" came into the world. It believed that it had to go behind existence in order to discover "in the

The Personality of Friedrich Nietzsche

eternal" the reasons for "good and evil." But with the "eternal," with the "beyond," Nietzsche had also to reject the "eternal" evaluation of "good and evil." Man has come into existence through the natural; and "good and evil" have come into existence with him. The creation of mankind is "good and evil." And deeper than the created is the creator. The "human being" stands "beyond good and evil." He has made the one thing to be good, the other to be evil. He may not let himself be chained through his former "good and evil." He can follow further the path of evolution which he has taken till now. From the worm he has become a human being; from man he can develop to the superman. He can create a new good and evil. He may "reevaluate" present day values. Nietzsche was torn from his work on *Umwertung aller Werte,* Transvaluation of All Values, through his spiritual darkness. The evolution of the worm to the human being was the idea which he had gained from the more recent natural science. He himself did not become a scientist; he had adopted the idea of evolution from others. For them it was a matter of the intellect; for him it became a matter of the heart. The others waged a spiritual battle against all old prejudices. Nietzsche asked himself how he could live with the new idea. *His* battle took place entirely within his own soul. He needed the further development to the superman in order to be able to bear mankind. Thus, by itself, in lonely heights, his sensitive spirit had to overcome the natural science which he had taken into himself. During his last creative period, Nietzsche tried to attain from reality itself what earlier he thought he could gain in illusion, in an ideal realm. Life is assigned a task which is firmly rooted in life, and yet leads over and above this life. In this immediate existence one cannot remain standing in real life, or in the life illuminated by natural science. In this life there also *must be suffering*. This remained Nietzsche's opinion. The "superman" is also a means to make life *bearable*. All this points to the fact that Nietzsche was born to "suffer from existence." His genius consisted in the searching for bases for consolation. The struggle for world conceptions has often engendered martyrs. Nietzsche has produced no new ideas for a world conception. One will always recognize that his genius does not lie in the production of new ideas. But he suffered deeply because of the thoughts surrounding him. In compensation for this suffering he found the enraptured tones of his *Zarathustra*. He became the *poet* of the new world conception; the hymns in praise of the "superman" are the personal, the *poetic* reply to the problems and results of the more recent natural science. All that the nineteenth century produced in ideas, would also have been produced without Nietzsche. In the eyes of the future he will not be considered an original philosopher, a founder of religions, or a prophet; for the future he will be a martyr of knowledge, who in poetry found words with which to express his suffering.

INDEX

A

accidents, 42
Achilles, 76
Aeschylus (525-456 B.C.), 13, 130, 142
aesthetic
    enjoyment, 79
    idealism, 111
    impression, 158
Alps, 46
Styrian, 14
Also Sprach Zarathustra, Nietzsche, 25, 39, 43, 45, 47, 50, 58, 68, 71, 98, 99, 101, 102, 104, 112, 114-15, 121, 137, 149, 169, 173, 184-5, 193, 195, 202, 209, 212
America, 11
Anaxagoras (500-428 B.C.), 195
Anaximander (611-547 B.C.), 195
ancestors, 140
Antichrist, Nietzsche, 113, 121, 148-9, 167-8, 170, 194, 201
Apollonian
    art, 128, 156, 157
    man, 13-14, 186
    soul condition, 205
    world conception, 128
Aristophanes (448-385 B.C.), 13
art
    Greek, 128, 156
    value of, 108, 111, 133-34
    views on, 77, 78, 79, 108-9, 165
artist, the, 76, 197
asceticism, 81 f., 86, 88, 111, 188

ascetics, 76
atheism, 89
athiest, 88, 89, 155

B

Bajadere, 85
baroque, 144
Basel, 186, 207
    University of, 17, 18, 20, 23, 28, 29, 182, 194, 204
Bayreuth, 21, 25
beauty, 79, 108-9, 128, 165, 167
Beethoven, Ludwig van (1770-1827), 144
believers, Nietzsche on, 42-3, 202
Berlin, 30, 34, 201
Bible, the, 82
Bizet, Georges (1838-1875), 109-10
Böcklin, Arnold (1827-1901), 203
Bonn, 186
    University of, 15
books, Nietzsche on his, 58-60, 173, 201-2
Borgia, Cesare (1476-1507), 166-67, 172
bourgeoise, 108, 123, 142
Brandes, Georg Morris Cohen (1842-1927), 29, 30, 47, 202, 203
Brentano, Franz (1838-1917), 26
Brockhaus, Prof. Hermann (1806-1877), 16
Burckhardt, Jacob Christoph (1818-1897), 18, 20, 23, 28, 29, 182, 194, 204

Index

C

camel, 72
Carmen, Bizet, 109
"categorical imperative," 95-6, 99, 100, 112
Cesare Borgia (1476-1507), 166-67, 172
child, 72
chorus, Greek tragic, 129
Christ, 65, 89, 113, 124, 148
Christianity, the spirit of, 82, 124, 148-9
Cistercian Abbey, 13
commandments, moral, 53, 144-45
Conrad, Michael Georg (1846-1927), 155, 171, 183, 185
conscience, 95-6, 99, 100, 105, 117
conscious motives, 117
consciousness, 118
Copenhagen, University of, 203
Cotta Publishing Company, 31
creativity, 138
criminal types, 119
criticism, professorial, 120
Crusaders, Christian, 52
culture, fundamental idea of, 137
Greek, 130
curative education, 27
cynicism, 63

D

dancer, Dionysian, 114-15
dancing, 128, 156
danger, 42
Darwin, Charles (1809-1882), 31, 187, 188
Darwinian literature, 174
democracy, 106, 108
Democritus (460-370 B.C.), 195
destiny, 98, 103
destruction, impulse to, 164, f.
Deutsche Theologie, die (quoted), 81-83
devil, the, 83
dialectic, 47, 183
Dilthey, Wilhelm (1833-1911), 198

Dionysian
  art, 128, 156, 193, 209
  creative spirit, 132, 133
  man, 113, 114, 118, 186
  soul condition, 206
  world conception, 128, 132
Dionysus, 130, 157, 167, 205
dithyrambic dramatist, 133
dramatic art, 129, 133, 157
dream, 93, 94
DuBois-Reymond, Emil (1818-1896), 88
Duhring, Eugen Karl (1833-1921), 161

E

eagle, 71, 184
earnestness, Apollonian, 114
Ecce Homo, Nietzsche, 155, 165, 171, 183
Eckermann, Johann Peter (1792-1854), 189
education, 27
  average, 144
  curative, 27
  true, 120, 134, 135
Egyptians, 163
Einbildungskraft und Wehnsinn (Dilthey), 198
Emerson, Ralph Waldo (1803-1882), 13, 34
Empedocles (490-430 B.C.), 195
Engadine, Swiss, 24
epic style, 156
Epicurus (342-270 B.C.), 79
"eternal return," 149, 161, 167, 175, 184-5
Eton, the German, 13
Euripides (480-406 B.C.), 129, 164
Europe, 46
evil, 45, 105, 106
  origin of, 99, 210, 211
evolution, 210, 211
existentialist poet, pre-, 193, 209

Index

F

factuality, fanatics of, 88
Fall Wagner, Der, Nietzsche, 29, 77-78, 110, 121, 164
family, idea of, 125
fantasy, moral, 117
Faust, Goethe, 26, 76, 108
Fichte, Johann Gottlieb (1762-1814), 13, 24, 32, 48, 93, 94, 95-97
  Bestimmung des Menschen, 94-97
  Ueber die Bestimmung des Gelehrten, 48
forgetting, 139
Fors Clavigera, Ruskin, 35
Franco-Prussian War, 1870, 19, 20, 46, 143
Frankfurt, 206
free person, the, 118, 123
Free Spirit, The, Nietzsche, 121, 167
free spirits, 44, 45, 89, 100, 104, 115
free thinkers, 43, 44, 53
"free will," theory of, 44
freedom, acting in, 117, 118
Freedom, Philosophy of, Steiner, 91, 117
French Riviera, 24
Fröhliche, Wissenschaft, Nietzsche, 52, 56, 57, 118, 147, 162, 169, 176

G

games, Greek festival, 157
Geburt der Trägodie, Nietzsche, 20, 46, 128, 130, 131, 156, 164
Genealogie der Moral, Nietzsche, 28, 39, 53, 76, 77, 81, 83-4, 89, 121
genius, the, 198
  of Nietzsche, discussed, 175
geometry, Steiner on, 18, 19, 92
German spirit, the, 46
Germania Club, the, 13
Germans, the, 170
Germany, 20, 21, 29, 30, 46
Geschichte der Renaissance in Italien, Burckhardt, 18
gestures, 128, 156
God, commandments of, 95
  denial of, 44
  existence of, 88
  image of, 66
  Will of, 53, 65
godless, Zarathustra the, 99
Goethe, Johann W. von (1749-1832), 12, 26, 27, 30, 34, 76, 108, 188-190
  As Father of a New Aesthetics, Steiner, 30
  Faust, 26, 76, 108
  scientific writings of, 27, 30
Society, Vienna, 30
Theory of Knowledge of, Steiner, 28
Goethe-Schiller Archives, Weimar, 30, 32
Goethes Weltanschauung, Steiner, 34
good and evil, 99, 101, 106, 111-12, 119
  origin of, 210-11
Götzendammerung, Nietzsche, 29, 39, 51, 58, 121, 132, 154, 163
Greece, ancient, 142, 191, 195, 196
Greek
  art, 128, 131
  chorus, 129
  culture, ancient, 130, 204, 207, 208
  myths, 129
  tragedy, 129, 131
Greeks, the ancient, 46, 131, 168, 195, 196
Grimm, Hermann (1840-1901), 31
Gustavus Adolphus (1594-1632), 12

H

Haeckel, Ernst Heinrich (1834-1919), 26, 31, 87
Hartmann, Eduard v. (1842-1906), 26, 30
health, Nietzsche on, 147
heat, mechanical theory of, 26

Hegel, Georg Wilhelm Friedrich (1770-1831), 109, 124
Heine, Heinrich (1797-1856), 185-6
Hell, 148
Hellenic, the, 196-7
Heraclitus (535-475 B.C.), 195, 205
Himalayas, 85
history, 137-141
historical being, 137
Hobbes, Thomas (1588-1679), 187
Holderlin, Johann C. F. (1770-1843), 142
Holy Spirit, the, 123-4
Homer (c. 10th Cent. B.C.), 76, 118
Homer & Classical Philology, Nietzsche, 17
hospital, 103
humor, 142
Hungary, 14, 18, 19

I

idea of beauty, 108, 109
idealism, German, 122
  moral, 62
idealists, 61, 65, 67, 74
ideals, 65, 75
Immoralist, The, Nietzsche, 121, 167
insane, the, 123
instincts, the, 115-116, 134
  slave of the, 117-118
intellect, the, 47, 52, 69, 91, 92, 94, 148
Italy, 18, 24
Ixion, the wheel of, 79

J

Jenseits von Gut und Böse, Nietzsche, 28, 30, 39, 48, 49, 54, 57, 91, 92, 103, 121, 142, 161-2, 170, 172, 187
Jew, one, 170
Juggernaut, 85
Jupiter, 190
justice, 106

K

Kant, Immanuel (1724-1804), 23, 24, 60, 79, 132
Kritik der reinen Vernunft, 23
Ketzerblut, Conrad (quoted), 155, 171, 183, 185
Kingdom of God, 148
Klopstock, Friedrich Gottlieb (1724-1803), 13
knowledge, 112, 126, 162
  impulse for, 91
  limits of (Kant), 58
  a process of, 91, 92
  theorists of, 91
Koegel, Fritz, 32, 40
Kraljevec, 14
Kürschner, Joseph (1853-1902), 27
Kursus der Philosophie, Duhring, 161

L

Laistner, Ludwig, 31
Landes-Schule, Pforta, 13, 15, 155
language, human, 133
laughing, Dionysian, 114
laws, 52, 65
Lehmann, Joseph, 34
Leipzig, 12, 23, 186
  University of, 16, 17
Leitfaden der Physiologischen Psychologie, Ziehen, 181
Lenau, Nicholas von (1802-1850), 125
Leopardi, Count Giacomo (1798-1837), 185-6, 187, 189
Library of World Literature, Cotta, 32
life, Nietzsche on, 187
  value of, 50
lion, 72
logic, Nietzsche and, 131-32, 154, 159
loneliness, Nietzsche on, 57
Lucerne, Lake of, 17
Luther, Martin (1483-1546), 82
lyric style, 156

M

Magazine for Literature, 34, 41
Malthus, Thomas Robert (1766-1834), 187
marriage, 125
martyrs, 212
mechanics, 161
memorial address for Nietzsche, 34, 201 f.
memory, 137
Menschliches Allzumenschliches, Nietzsche, 22, 25, 40, 146, 160, 165, 209
Metz, 46
Meysenberg, Baroness v., 22, 25
Meysenbug, Malvida v., 159-60
Midas, King, 130
Milan, 186
monks, 19, 52-53
moral fantasy, Steiner on, 117
morality, fount of, 96
Morgenröte, Nietzsche, 24, 42, 100, 146, 182
Moritz, St., 182
motives, conscious, 117
music, 76-7, 133, 156, 157, 193, 209
Nietzsche on, 109, 110, 193, 209
musical art, 156
myths, Greek, 129

N

Napoleon I (1769-1821), 23
nature, laws of, 90
natural science, 87, 160, 161, 194, 204, 210, 211, 212
Naumberg, 12, 182, 186
Neudörfl, 18, 19
New Testament, 170
Nietzsche Archives, 32, 41
  Elizabeth Förster, 13, 28, 32, 33, 41, 155, 183, 184, 191, 193
  genius of, 175-6
  Library of, 33
  Pastor, 12

Nietzsche, Works by:
  Also Sprach Zarathustra, 25, 39, 43, 45, 47, 50, 58, 68, 71, 98, 99, 101, 102, 104, 112, 114-15, 121, 137, 149, 169, 173, 184-85, 193, 195, 202, 209, 212
  Antichrist, 113, 121, 148-49, 167, 168, 170, 194, 201
  Ecce Homo, 155, 165, 171, 183
  Der Fall Wagner, 29, 77-78, 110, 121, 164
  Free Spirit, The, 121, 167
  Fröhliche Wissenschaft, 52, 56, 57, 118, 147, 162, 169, 176
  Geburt der Trägodie, 20, 46, 128, 130, 131, 156, 164
  Genealogie der Moral, 28, 39, 53, 76, 77, 81, 83, 84, 89, 121
  Götzendammerung, 29, 39, 51, 58, 121, 132, 154, 163, 196
  Immoralist, The, 121, 167
  Jenseits von Gut und Böse, 28, 30, 39, 48-9, 54, 57, 91, 92, 103, 121, 142, 161-2, 170, 172, 187
  Menschliches Alzumenschliches, 22, 25, 40, 146, 160, 165, 209
  Morgenröte, 24, 42, 100, 146, 182
  Nietzsche contra Wagner 110
  Nutzen und Nachteil der Historie, 20, 138-141
  Schopenhauer als Erzieher, 20, 45, 56, 134, 135, 137-38, 206
  David Strauss, 20, 46, 143
  Unzeitgemässe Betrachtungen, 20
  Umwertung aller Werte, 167, 211
  Wagner in Bayreuth, 20, 132, 133, 159, 164, 193, 209
  Wanderer und sein Schatten, 146, 182
  Wille zur Macht, 121, 149
Nïëzky family, 12
nihilism, aesthetic, 111
  philosophical, 95, 97, 165
Ninth Symphony, Beethoven, 144
nothingness, belief in, 94-5, 97, 111, 126, 149

Index

O

Olympic Gods, 131, 167
Opera & Drama, Wagner, 76
oracle, ancient Greek, 195
orthodoxy, Christian, 45, 123

P

Paradise, 148
Paris, 21, 28
Parmenides (c. 475 B.C.), 195, 205
Parsifal, Wagner, 25
Patagonian, 145
pathological, the, 164, 177, 181, 187, 197, 198
peace, 73, 102
Persians, ancient, 195
pessimism, 184
Philistine, the bourgeois, 142-144
philosophers, 49, 51, 53, 54, 59, 60, 66, 79-80, 109, 136, 138, 146, 162, 183, 192, 195, 197, 212
philosophical nihilism, 95
Philosophy of Freedom, Steiner, 32, 91, 117
physics, history of, 26
Pilate, Pontius (Governor 26-36? A.D.), 170
Pilatus, Mount, 17
Plato (427-347 B.C.), 13, 191
Pope, the, 167
Pottsach, 14, 15
power, 49-51, 54, 63, 91, 102, 106, 125-6, 148
pride, 56, 71, 74, 148
priests, ascetic ideals of, 81f., 83, 86
Protestant, a faithful, 123
psychiatry, 153 f., 175
psychology, 153 f., 164, 171, 175, 177, 181, 186
psychopathology, 153 f., 176
punishment, 105

R

Railway, South Austrian, 14, 18
Ranke, Leopold v. (1795-1886), 13
Rée, Dr. Paul, 22, 25, 40, 159, 160
reflection, the art of, 157
Reformation, the, 13
Reitlinger, Edmund, 26
religion, Neitzsche no founder of, 43
Renaissance, the, 191
revenge, 107
Revue des Deux Mondes, Paris, 21
Rheinisches Museum, 17
Richter, Hans (1843-1916), 21
Jean Paul Friedrich (1763-1825), 31
Ring des Niebelungen, Wagner, 21
Ritschel, Friedrich Wilhelm 1806-1876), 15, 17, 20, 204
Riviera, French, 24
Röcken near Leipzig, 12, 34
Romans, ancient, 168, 170, 195, 196
romanticism, 159
Rostock, University of, 32
Ruskin, John (1819-1900), 35

S

Salomé, Lou Andreas, 25, 40
scepticism, philosophical, 163, 194
Schelling, Friedrich W. J. von (1775-1854), 108
Schiller, Friedrich (1759-1805), 12, 26, 30, 32
schizophrenia, 190
Schlegel, August Wilhelm (1767-1845), 13
Schopenhauer, Artur (1788-1860), 16, 23 32, 42, 45, 56, 76-78, 82, 111, 122, 126, 127, 132-136, 157-8, 160, 164-5, 184, 195, 204, 206
als Erzieher, Nietzsche, 20, 45, 56, 134, 135, 137-8, 206
Welt als Wille und Vorstellung, 16, 78, 85, 126, 157
Schröer, Karl Julius, 26, 27
Schulpforta, 13, 15, 155, 186
Schuré, Edouard (1840-1929), 21-22
science, modern, 86-89
sculpture, 156
seasons of the year, 186

Index

self-torture, 85
serpent, 71, 184
Seven Wise Ones of Greece, 196
Shakespeare, William (1564-1616), 13
shepherd, 69, 84
Silenus, the wise, 130, 205
sin, 82, 83
singing, 128
Slav, 21
slaves, 53, 107, 118, 172, 173
"snake death," Zarathustra, 104
Socrates (469-399 B.C.), 51, 129, 130, 131, 132, 163, 183, 191, 195, 204-5, 206, 211, 212
Socratic school, 197
Sophie of Saxony, Archduchess, 30
Sorrento, 22
Sphinx, the, 48
Stein, Ludwig, 119
Steiner, Rudolf, Works referred to:
  Goethe as Founder of a New Aesthetics, 30
  Goethe's Conception of the World, 34
  Philosophy of Freedom, 32, 91, 117
  Theory of Knowledge in Goethe's World Conception, 28, 39
  Truth and Science, 26, 32, 91
Stendhal, (Marie Henri Beyle) (1783-1842), 79
Stirner, Max (Johann Caspar Schmidt) (1806-1856), 122
  quoted, 123-126
Stoics, the   124
Strauss, David Friedrich (1808-1874), 142-143
  (by Nietzsche), 20, 46, 143
  Alte und Neue Glaube, 143-145
Strindberg, Johan August 1849-1912), 29
"struggle for existence" (Darwin), 174, 187, 188
sufferers, dominion over, 84
suffering, 85, 102, 212

superman (Nietzsche's concept of), 40, 64, f., 68, 69, 70, 112, 126, 137, 147-8, 166-7, 174, 211, 212
sympathy, 102, 103, 104

T

Tacitus, Publius Cornelius (55-120 A.D.), 13
Taine, Hyppolyte Adolphe (1828-1893), 28, 29
Tautenberg, 25, 186
teacher, the right, 134-5
Technische Hochschule, Vienna, 24, 26
temples, Egyptian, 163
Testament, the New, 170
Thales (640-546 B.C.), 195, 205
"thing in itself," 126
tragedy, origin of Greek, 129, 158-59
Triebschen estate, Wagner's, 17, 207
Tristram Shandy (novel, 1749-67)
  by Lawrence Sterne, 13
truth, 89
Truth, and Science, Steiner, 26, 32, 91
truth, sense of, 154, 159, 163
  value of, 47-8, 49
Turin, 30, 186
tyrants, 53

U

Umwertung aller Werte, Nietzsche, 167, 211
untruth, 48, 154, 159, 163
Unzeitgemässe Betrachtungen, Nietzsche, 20

V

value, intrinsic, 64-5, 107-8, 147
Venice, 25, 186
victory, 102, 106
Vienna, 24, 30, 31, 34
  University of, 26
virtue, 70, 72-3

Index

Vischer, Friedrich Theodore (1807-1887), 26, 142
Voltaire (Francois Marie Arouet de) (1694-1778), 189

W

Wagner Cosima (1837-1930), 17
Richard (1813-1883), 16, 17, 20, 21, 25, 29, 76-8, 110, 111, 122, 132, 133, 159, 164-5, 190-193, 204, 206-209
Wagner in Bayreuth, Nietzsche, 20, 132-3, 159, 164, 193, 209
Wagner, der Fall, Nietzsche, 29, 77-8, 110, 121, 164
Wahle, Richard, 86
Wahrheit und Wissenschaft, Steiner, 26, 32, 91
Wanderer und sein Schatten, Nietzsche, 146, 182
war, the strong love, 102
weather, Nietzsche and, 42, 186
Weimar, 30, 31, 32, 34, 41
Edition of Goethe's Works, 30
Werther, Goethe, 142

Western culture, 48, 165, 205
Wiener-Neustadt, 19
Wilamowitz-Moellendorf, Ulrich v. (1848-1931), 20
will, the eternal (Fichte on), 96-7, 99
Wille zur Macht, Nietzsche, 121, 149
willing, the art of, 157
Wise Ones, Seven (of Greece), 196
words, the meaning of, 133
work, Nietzsche on, 108
Wörth, 46

Y

youth, German, 20

Z

Zarathustra, Also Sprach, Nietzsche, 25, 39, 43, 45, 47, 50, 58, 68, 71, 98, 99, 101, 102, 104, 112, 114-15, 121, 137, 149, 169, 173, 184-5, 193, 195, 202, 209, 212
Ziehen, Theodor, 181
Zimmerman, Robert, 26

www.ingramcontent.com/pod-product-compliance
Lightning Source LLC
Chambersburg PA
CBHW032250150426
43195CB00008BA/398